Th

"In the brilliant pantheon of new Philadelphia writers . . . Nathaniel Popkin has already established himself as the dreamcatcher. In *The Possible City* he catches the moment when Philadelphia dreaming seems palpably plausible. He has the nerve to see the city as the ruin it is, fallen from a majesty New York will never know, and the passion to see the city as the wonder it remains. He is at once the poet of our palsy and the conjurer of the magic that comes of calling on a melancholy and audacious past to summon a glory that might be."

—Mike Zuckerman,
Professor of History, University of Pennsylvania

"Popkin is emerging as Philadelphia's literary voice. Using the insights and experiences of our lives, he is showing us what Philadelphia can become. His sensitive portrayal of the modern city linked to the elevating vision of its founder provides the guideposts for our future imaginings. From the grand to what's outside our door, this book helps us gain an insight to a word on the lips of all Philadelphians—'potential.'"

—Sam Katz

"[In this] lovely book Popkin has written an evocative and provocative portrait of a great but flawed city. It is defiant and fierce and filled with the power and potential of urban life. It should be read by anyone who loves cities and dreams of making them better."

—Richard C. Schragger,
Professor of Law, University of Virginia

THE POSSIBLE CITY

Exercises in
Dreaming Philadelphia

Nathaniel Popkin

CAMINO BOOKS, INC.

PHILADELPHIA

for Mom and Dad

Manufactured in the United States of America

1 2 3 4 5   11 10 09 08

Library of Congress Cataloging-in-Publication Data

Popkin, Nathaniel R.
  The possible city : exercises in dreaming Philadelphia / Nathaniel Popkin.
    p. cm.
  ISBN 978-1-933822-18-1 (alk. paper)
  1. Cities and towns—Pennsylvania—Philadelphia—History. 2. City
planning—Pennsylvania—Philadelphia—History. 3. Philadelphia
(Pa.)—Social life and customs. 4. Philadelphia (Pa.)—History. I. Title.
HT393.P42P67 2008
307.1′2160974811—dc22   2008028632

All photographs courtesy of R. Bradley Maule

Cover and interior design: Jan Greenberg

This book is available at a special discount on bulk purchases
for promotional, business, and educational use.

Publisher
Camino Books, Inc.
P.O. Box 59026
Philadelphia, PA 19102

www.caminobooks.com

Preface

MY EARLIER BOOK, *SONG OF THE CITY*, concludes with a short chapter, "Perchance to Dream," in which I invent an imaginary planning commission to dream of the possible city. What follows in this book is the culmination of several more years of exploring Philadelphia, talking with some of its most interesting and knowledgeable citizens, and reflecting on what this place is and might be. Many readers recognize that "The Possible City" is the title of a column I write on the website PhillySkyline.com and, indeed, many of the ideas in this book are derived from those columns as well as guest editorial columns in the *City Paper* and material prepared for and presented in other publications.

It's important to see *The Possible City* as one step in a long process that began before *Song of the City*, when as a young planner I began to feel this city's most tangible potential. It continues beyond this book. *The Possible City*, which is a joint project with PhillySkyline.com's editor Brad Maule, has only just begun an exploration of the tensions that define Philadelphia's now 60-year-long journey from industrial power to something else, still not understood or realized. The election as mayor of the enormously capable Michael Nutter only seems to underscore the timeliness of this work.

I owe enormous gratitude to Brad, whose photographs illustrate this book and who has been willing to open his wise and witty website to my writings and ideas. He has allowed me as a writer to connect with readers in profound and edifying ways. This process has been amplified at the *City Paper*, where former editor Duane Swierczynski and current editor Brian Howard have graciously allowed me to take part in their forum. I am lucky and honored that

Edward Jutkowitz, the longtime publisher of Camino Books and first to publish the collected commentaries of former *Philadelphia Inquirer* columnist Steve Lopez, has agreed to add *The Possible City* to his catalog. It's a great home for the book.

The Possible City is a product of Philadelphia University, where as writer-in-residence I have been given, among a terrific faculty and a creative student body, a chance to air and discuss ideas and time to write the essays that form this book. The School of Liberal Arts and the Office of Academic Affairs invented this residency, and a great deal of gratitude is owed to Liberal Arts Dean Marion Roydhouse and (sadly outgoing) director of the writing program John Eliason, and to Jim Savoie, the Assistant Vice President of Academic Affairs, who has been constant in his support for the campus projects I pursue. Class and studio time with faculty and students in architecture and industrial design, including my close compatriot Josh Owen, directly informed the content of this book.

The painter and builder Jeff McMahon has illuminated, in altogether novel ways, a poetry of the city street. The publisher Paul Dry has been a wise rabbi to me this year, helping to shape and structure this work and keeping me focused on the particular Philadelphia reality.

The Arcadia University historian Peter Siskind, my most faithful reader and friend, has had a part in every step of this book, from our long walks discussing the infinite facets of the urban realm to the heavy lifting of editing these essays. Without Peter the observations that inform this book would never have taken form, either as raw ideas or as something more cogent and enjoyable to read.

Every ounce of my gratitude goes finally to my wife Rona Buchalter, who with unvarying and incomprehensible patience has read and improved every word in every essay, story, and book I've ever written. She makes all things possible.

Contents

INTRODUCTION

What is Philadelphia?

IN PHILADELPHIA, IMAGINING A NEW CITY IS A SINGULAR act of citizenship. When we look at Philadelphia, we see what might be. That tendency to see possibility around every corner comes in response to two sensations. The first is the recognition of *what isn't*. Here is the cold understanding of what, in comparison to other cities, Philadelphia lacks. The second is the awareness of *what was*. We're reminded of this ceaselessly, of the city's founding ideals, of its political, economic, and industrial prominence. In Philadelphia, William Penn sought a different kind of city, one guided by principles of tolerance and love. These are active principles in Philadelphia, and we turn to them especially in times of crisis. They help us see what might be.

We dream so intensely because a more satisfying city feels ever so tantalizingly close. We dream too because as hard and unforgiving as Philadelphia is, it also relents; any one of us it seems can mold it to the shape of our desires.

It's all there in the ruins we call the contemporary city.

With a city full of dreamers, imagine how many Philadelphias there are, how many ideas, renderings, concepts, capstones, thesis projects, studio designs, abstract scribbles, master plans, renewal plans, redevelopment plans, green plans, sustainability strategies, waterfront designs, how many dreams and ideas have been projected at scale across a plotted map of this city—and therefore just how many possible cities there are. The architect Louis Kahn probably could have filled the entire 1:1 scale 135 square miles with Availabilities, Rooms, Courts, Forums, Civic Centers, and Inspirations neatly drawn and never built, only to exist as a tacked-up netherworld, a colossal, ever-growing what-might-have-been with a steady population and plastic bags that don't swirl ceaselessly in the wind.

For many architects and planners, especially, these possible cities blur the line between reality and the imagination. Anthologies of Kahn's work are replete with the un-built, elaborate exercises in dreaming that seem almost indistinguishable from the things of permanence that were erected in due order.

Of all the recent changes in human civilization, few compare to the global rate of urbanization. In 1961, when the farsighted city planner and scholar (and colleague of Kahn at the University of Pennsylvania's newly formed Graduate School of Fine Arts) Lewis Mumford wrote *The City in History*, he was able to do so without considering the cities of Asia and South America. That would not be possible today. As Mike Davis notes in the introduction to *Planet of Slums*, "In 1950 there were 86 cities in the world with a population of more than one million; today there are 400, and by 2015 there will be at least 550."

So what's Philadelphia in a world of Hefei, Xintai, Jamshedpur, Asansol, Karaj, and Taegu? Number 129 and dropping. The dropping—that is Philadelphia's unending struggle to retain a sense of relevance in a world that feels so vast and decentralized—colors our dreams. The dropping infects the city with a sense of loss; at times the loss becomes grief and then pain.

All this seems to leave Philadelphia dangerously near the edge of the contemporary American narrative. The United States has the third largest urban population in the world, behind China and India. But after a familiar cycle—growth, industrialization, immigration, decentralization, deindustrialization, and suburbanization—the U.S. is left with a sprawling urban form, sharply different from the concentrated cities of the rest of world. At present, large, dense cities like Philadelphia account for only about 7 percent of the U.S. population—22 million people—the lowest percentage since 1830.

In Philadelphia, industrialization began in earnest around 1830 and mass immigration followed, so that by 1900 this city was the tenth largest city in the world. Then, there was one Philadelphian for every 50 Americans from other cities and towns; at present, due to the nation's expansion and the city's population decline (by 25 percent since 1950), that ratio is one in 250. Put another way, a contemporary group of 50 people isn't likely to include someone from our Wingohocking or Passyunk neighborhoods.

What then is a Philadelphia in a country whose heart feels like it is in Sunbelt cities like Charlotte, Phoenix, Las Vegas, and Houston? That's something this city has been trying to figure out since the mid-20th century, when the postindustrial period began. Philadelphia ever since has been searching for a reason to be. We're still searching, our dreams hindered—but also fed—by the ruins of a more populous place.

It can be hard to tell if anyone else cares—not just about Philadelphia, of course, but about all the cities of the Rustbelt. Given the relatively low proportion of Americans who live in dense cities, Washington hasn't articulated a coherent urban policy since the mid-1990s, when the Clinton administration funded empowerment zones. But even that was halfhearted, a realigning of programs rather than a concerted new investment in our old cities. Many commentators have noted that urban issues have not gained interest during the 2008 presidential election season.

The political ambivalence is hampered further by an emphasis on personal wealth. America remains one of the lowest-taxed rich nations in the world, a posture that limits the national capacity to invest in the collective, urban realm, from infrastructure to education.

Yet strangely, and surprisingly to many, parts of Philadelphia have benefited substantially from the further tax cuts implemented by the administration of George W. Bush. Indeed, from smallish firms like Walnut Street Capital, the developer of the proposed colossal American Commerce Center (at 1,500 feet it will be one of the tallest buildings in the nation), to major institutions like the University of Pennsylvania, with a trove of super-rich donors, some in Philadelphia have been able to align profit with a tangible, and exciting, urban resurgence.

Much of this real estate investment—it is difficult to visualize just how much has taken place since the mid-1990s—has made Philadelphia nicer for many. It has most noticeably fed a certain kind of urbane street life. In Philadelphia particularly, it has also helped to maintain the city's traditional array of light industrial and craft workshops. Spending by the rich on urban real estate preserves craft industry, notably by embellishing skills in carpentry, building preservation, cabinetmaking, masonry, sculpture, and metalwork, and by providing a market for specialized merchants of lighting, flooring, and other building materials.

Concentrated wealth carefully aimed to the urban streetscape enables the Philadelphia Museum of Art to expand, the Barnes Foundation to move in from its suburban location, the Jewish Museum to open. This is no small thing. The result of the investment is pervasive, substantial, and far-reaching. After about 30 years of incremental but not insignificant investments in certain neighborhoods, this latest push has Philadelphia adopting a new outlook. The center of the city especially looks good, feels larger, and seems livelier. Out-migration continues as it does in every city, but in-migration has increased. Now foreign-born immigrants again comprise a significant portion of the population, a key indicator of health for an American city. People are coming, and that, in turn, expands the city's vision.

One result of this is a tangible shift in our urban expectations. The movement against waterfront casinos has revealed a new buzzword: transparency. The necessity to address global warming has given us another: sustainability, this one packed with the fertile loam of a million new utopias. The election of the pragmatic Michael Nutter as mayor has many Philadelphians believing that something might finally come of it.

But we well know that the act of dreaming isn't the act of building; nor, even under the best circumstances, do the vast majority of dreams come to reality. The present paradigm rewards the rich—so much so that on many streets a desperate fatalism seems to have descended, and, like a low-pressure system, it sits no matter the hopeful rhetoric otherwise. At times it feels intractable, engendering not only hopelessness but a defensive pride. In some neighborhoods that pride is wielded to assert control—to erect boundaries—enforcing a parochial outlook, denying the city its hope for elevation, and leaving little, if anything, to show for it.

Still it is worth remembering that for every Mary Brown, longtime West Philadelphia neighborhood organizer whose sensible hopes for 52nd Street were ultimately plowed under by the brutal disorder of poverty and inadequate public investment, there is Shane Claiborne, the visionary you'll find in Chapter 2, whose singular sprit has infected the blocks around Kensington and Allegheny. For every Foxwoods Casino, a mindless giveaway to well-positioned developers, there is Cedar Park, the pizza slice of public space just east of 52nd Street that was lovingly rebuilt last year after the completion of a well-honed process of community design. Our dreams remain particularly defiant and fierce, and a great many of them endure. Certain urban observers call this irrational. What's a Philadelphia in contemporary America? An anachronism no more. But others, including University of Virginia law professor and former Philadelphian Richard Schragger, suggest that cities, uniquely, drive the creation of wealth and culture. Schragger says cities therefore ought to assert a native economic power, doing so in part by exploiting the gray area of law that exists in our federal system. Not unfamiliar with revolutionary posturing, Philadelphia has done just so throughout its history, recently by defying Pennsylvania state law on gun control, but also with political ambitions about trade, energy, and the environment.

But will political and legal defiance—the erection of gun control at the local level, for example—turn *the city that might be* into *the city that is*? It will help, if only as a practical matter, to solve a local problem—but also by asserting power. Defiance feels good. It builds confidence.

It doesn't, however, rebuild neighborhoods or piece a city back together. I offer here what I hope is a useful tool. A current University of Pennsylvania professor of architecture, Winka Dubbeldam, has noted a difference between architecture that functions and architecture that performs. In thinking about cities, the difference between the two concepts is telling. Philadelphia, indeed, functions. It has altogether resisted paralysis—no small feat considering the extent of loss and decline. But it rarely performs. By that I mean it doesn't entertain, dazzle, inspire, show off, cohere, or elevate; it rarely makes one feel great.

Imagine, for a moment, the difference. I'll take a ready example. Philadelphia has a large transit system called SEPTA (Southeastern Pennsylvania Transportation Authority). The system provides about one million rides a day throughout the region. It does so somewhat ably, and service is improving. In other words, it functions. But its only ambition is to function—and that function is narrowly defined. A former SEPTA general manager said the agency's job was no more than to move people from point A to point B. Here, exposed, is the city that isn't. All over the world, and not that far from home, transit systems perform. They do so, quite literally, often by providing musical entertainment (the MTA in New York auditions talent); they do so by providing for all kinds of passenger needs; they do so by an ease of legibility that feeds the imagination; they do so with station architecture that inspires, that integrates with the streetscape, that elevates the sensation of travel; they do so also by allowing the passenger to linger if he likes, to explore, to wander. SEPTA, which does few of those things, is an example of the city that was. Its system is really the cobbled remains of a handful of transit companies that flourished in another era.

Between the two, the city that isn't and the city that was, we come to see the city that might be. Here, then, is the only possibility. A Philadelphia that is meaningful to its citizens, to America and the rest of the world, will be a Philadelphia that performs—in profound and particular ways.

THE POSSIBLE CITY

CHAPTER 1

(Con)Founding Ideals

ON A WARM DAY IN EARLY JULY, I TAKE MY YOUNG SON Isaak to the woods along the Wissahickon Creek. The creek, which cuts a gorge through the northwest part of the city, near Germantown, eventually flows to the Schuylkill River. It is Philadelphia's most wild and sacred territory, made famous in 1843 by Edgar Allan Poe:

> Its banks are generally, indeed almost universally, precipitous, and consist of high hills, clothed with noble shrubbery near the water, and crowned at a greater elevation, with some of the most magnificent forest trees of America...The immediate shores, however, are of granite, sharply defined or moss-covered, against which the pellucid water lolls in its gentle flow, as the blue waves of the Mediterranean upon the steps of her palaces of marble. Occasionally in front of the cliffs, extends a small definite plateau of richly herbaged land, affording the most picturesque position for a cottage and garden which the richest imagination could conceive.

Poe's travelogue, *Morning on the Wissahiccon*, ends with him spotting an animal he thinks is an elk posing on a rock. It may have been the rock we now call Mom Rinker's Rock. Isaak and I are headed there. We are on a quest.

It is a sultry day not unlike the one Poe describes. The air is fragrant, moist, metallic. We enter the woods from Park Drive and work our way slowly into the woods. Following the well-

marked trail, we shimmy and climb through small rock forma-
tions and cross a short concrete culvert, then come upon the famous rock. Isaak takes quickly to pretending he is in a scene in
Peter Pan. I wind around the famous rock.

"Can I go up?" eventually he wonders.

I guide him up the narrow trail and shortly we arrive at the
founder's feet. There it is, carved in the plinth of Herman Kirn's
1883 sculpture of William Penn: TOLERATION. The only offering is a worn, wooden, heart-shaped flag circa 1976. I can't
take my eyes off the word. Isaak, now bored, starts down, and
left alone, I do something almost impossibly uncharacteristic: I
put my fingers to my lips, stare across the gorge into the trees
opposite, and then place them on the letters of the word. How
odd and wonderful is the placement of this sculpture, hidden in
the copse and weeds, invisible to most. This is what it must feel
like to stumble upon a Buddha, or a Hindu god, in some lost
Asian forest. And yet, like the Alexander Stirling Calder statue
of Penn that towers above the city atop City Hall, Penn—and his
ideas—takes prominence. If this sounds messianic, then it
makes sense why standing atop the gorge, in one of the few
places in Philadelphia where it is possible to gain elevation, I was
so moved.

It was a prayer, I suppose, that Penn's vision would endure;
that our grappling with the singular cause of plurality would
make us a better people. In the first chapter of his book,
Metropolitan Philadelphia, Steven Conn gives us a beautiful exege-
sis on Philadelphia and "the echoes of William Penn." The historian calls Penn's "holy experiment" the longest-running
utopian dream. He says we uniquely carry forth the principle: in
a world of ethnic strife, we hold in our hand a possible other way.
But far more than the hope that Philadelphia can prove mean-

ingful to the wider world, the experience at Mom Rinker's Rock is instructive about place and self-identity. I had made a pilgrimage—in so doing a confirmation, an act of love.

Wisteria grows beneath the brick and the white marble portico and the straight white columns of the old hospital, the first hospital. Its flowers of bleached indigo dangle like the ears of a poodle, its thick hidden trunks like the legs of the dog, erect yet languorous, intelligent yet reticent, luxurious yet carefully restrained. The landscape planners who planted the garden must have known something of the aristocracy of flora, for they placed the wisteria at the center, coolly flanking the formal entrance. From this perch it pretends to take no notice of the more garish fuchsia coat of the azaleas, the searing lips of the tulips, the silver coat of the Tin Man, nor the face of the woman with thick curly hair who has come to pray.

The scene I describe is from a photograph taken by PhillySkyline.com's editor Brad Maule, part of a photo essay ostensibly about the colors of spring's mid-Atlantic palate. The woman kneels with her back to the camera; though we wish to, we can't see her expression. Can it be she is praying? Her arms quite clearly rest on the chains that protect the sculpture and the tulips that surround it, and her back is arched as if she is looking up to solicit help. It isn't the Tin Man before her, of course, though in the 1774 lead sculpture by John Bacon the Elder, William Penn strikes a notable resemblance to Jack Haley in *The Wizard of Oz.*

Penn had a lot of heart, and that's the point. Philadelphia's founder sought not to conquer but to befriend, not to coerce but to free, not to close doors but to open them. He taught and attempted to implement principles of love and respect for all. Listen to the 19th-century journalist George Lippard, editor of the *Quaker City Weekly* and close companion of Poe, in his column of October 6, 1849: "It was a glorious day when the slaves of all nations met upon this soil and saw their rude homes, the palaces of the poor, rise through the trees of wilderness. A great day when William Penn, standing on the soil, beheld the exiles of every land encircle him and girdle his open heart with a band of brothers."

In that early Philadelphia, political, legal, cultural, and moral boundaries gave way under the incremental waves of trade, commerce, and a guiding tolerance. In the open city, speakers of German, Spanish, Portuguese, French, English, and various native languages mixed freely. Here the earliest abolitionists mingled with black and female entrepreneurs, and women found in their new liberty unprecedented sexual freedom and power. It was a fertile moment. The documents and ideas this Philadelphia produced—the Germantown anti-slavery manifesto, the first constitution of Pennsylvania, Thomas Paine's *Common Sense*, the Declaration of Independence—are the markings of a society so open it seethed with brilliant possibility. And thus our city harbored an awakening and an enlightenment all at once.

Penn's doctrine resonated from the start, and still does. No other American city, says the historian Steven Conn, is so closely coupled with a founder and no founder with the principles of a religion. Critically, they are secular principles—brotherly love and tolerance—desperately meaningful in the rough, pluralistic, and often balkanized city we inhabit today. Perhaps that's why, more than three centuries later, they endure. We—all of us—thrown together in this most intimate of cities, are forced to negotiate difference, forced daily to confront the consequences of poverty and ignorance, forced to wonder if, at the end of the day, Penn's utopia will ever be possible. Tolerance presents itself as another beguiling dream.

It's a collective dream, to be sure, but having observed Philadelphians facing Penn's ideals for two decades, I have come to realize that the feelings they engender are deeply, surprisingly personal. Looking again at Maule's photograph of the Pennsylvania Hospital garden, it is unsettling to see a person in an American city praying in such a public manner. In a country where in religious matters the acceptance of an inner light has often seemed more authentic than ritual and performance, few act religiously in public. This isn't the case in much of the world. In the moonlike Mexican town of Mineral de Pozos, I once watched a woman with a baby in her arms, and kneeling in the same manner as the woman beneath the sculpture of William Penn, crawl upright on her knees the length of about three city blocks—and uphill—to the town cathedral. Her son laid out a small rug, which she crawled over; he picked it up and placed it in front of her again and so on until she made it all the way. Hers was an act of courage and humility. I gather but am unsure that the woman kneeling before William Penn, that most loving father, sought not to prostrate herself but to gain from the founder's strength of character and vision. What's clear is that a man who promoted a priestless religion that eschews idolatry has become our patron saint. The woman prays and Penn, looking down toward her, points with his right hand to his charter, which he holds out with his left. Here Philadelphia, he says, may these principles always guide you.

After more than three centuries some of us still hope they will. Contemporary Philadelphia is pluralistic and complex, a thorough amalgam of ideas, instincts, cultures, and points of view. Penn has something to tell us.

In *The City in History*, Lewis Mumford calls this intersection—a pluralistic city facing a singular ideal—"Venice versus Utopia." Here he pits the fictional Utopia of Thomas More against the accumulated and yet singular genius of Venice. Penn based his ideas for Philadelphia in part on More's Utopia, most evidently in the careful and rational plan that provided for gardens and orchards. Indeed, what strikes Mumford about Amaurote, the capital of the island of Utopia, is the uniform spatial design, allowing for the optimal personal connection to a garden. Amaurote, Mumford says, "is four-square in plan, on a tidal river, like London, to bring the boats in from the sea. The streets, twenty feet wide, are well laid out both for traffic and to avoid the winds. Every house has both a street door and a garden door...Each Utopian city is divided into four squares...." It appears the very description of Penn's Green Country Towne. Mumford also sees hints of the kind of equality, sameness ("Quaker drab"), and collective, negotiated control imagined by William Penn.

But Penn's utopian ideal—that his city would be a place of toleration—immediately opened the city to everyone. It wasn't ever meant to stay a Quaker city (Penn made the founding of the Anglican Christ Church a condition of his charter). And so, before the end of the 17th century, the process of amalgamation had already begun, precisely what Mumford says is the genius of Venice. "In short, the plan of Venice was no static design, embodying the needs of a single generation, arbitrarily ruling out the possibilities of growth, re-adaptation, change: rather, here was continuity in change, and unity emerging from complex order." Piazza San Marco, in particular, is "the product of cumulative urban purposes, modified by circumstance, function, and time: organic products that no human genius could produce in a few months over a drafting board."

This messy, adaptive, naturally evolving Venice is—perhaps without certain aspects of genius and unity—an apt description of our city today. "But who would exchange Venice for the dreary regimentation and uniformity of Amaurote?" asks Mumford. "And yet who would exchange the civic decencies of Amaurote for the secretive tyranny, the festering suspicions and hatreds, the assassinations of character, the felonious assaults and murders that underlay the prosperous trade and the festive art of Venice?"

So it seems we live at the intersection of the two cities today: our Venice stimulating, our Utopia chastening; our Venice a vivid accumulation of architecture, art, and landscape design, our Utopia an endless sea of endless blocks of even brick row-houses; our Venice filthy, our Utopia well-ordered; our Venice, it seems, a violent reality, our Utopia a prayerful yowl. Which is Philadelphia? On any given day, in any particular section of the city, one might encounter both—or one, quite a bit more force-fully than the other.

"Why do they call this the City of Brotherly Love?" His voice forlorn, his eyes pained, these are the words of José Gonzalez. Sitting on the stoop of his family's house on Pennhurst Street, he is speaking to Stephanie Farr, a reporter for the *Daily News*. The evening before, a Saturday night in the middle of the summer, Gonzalez's nephew Luis Navarro was riding his new green and white motorized dirt bike down a wooded lane in Tacony Creek Park on nearby Wyoming Avenue. The boy, 16, was shot and killed, his bike taken. On the dresser in his bedroom inspectors found a completed ap-plication for employment at Burlington Coat Factory. His mother, who had purchased the bike, had a nervous break-down and was taken to Einstein Hospital.

"Why do they call this the City of Brotherly Love?" On such a night it's a question we all of us ask, for a murder like this sends Philadelphia, desperate for an explanation, in search of its founder. But do Penn's ideals matter on streets replete with injustice and ruled by the happy trigger? Or do they simply effect—every time there is a senseless act of violence—a numbing and repetitive melancholy? Wouldn't it be easier and more honest to disown those ideals along with William Penn, Thomas Paine, the early German Quakers, and all those since who have attempted to reconcile Venice with Utopia? After all, Philadelphia has over the centuries lost its political and economic status; why not declare the experiment over and give up the ideals, too? And while we're at it, change the city's name. (Can you imagine the focus groups it would take to do so?) Even in Venice, the murder of a 16-year-old who is riding his bike in a city park would be devastating, a terrible loss, but what a relief not to have to call into question the moral foundations of the city. Why make a murder spree into the condemnation of the entire community?

The only answer is, *We're not Venice.* For that matter, we're not Detroit or St. Louis, Boston, or New York either. A burden or not, Philadelphia was invented to prove that human beings can live together peacefully. To give up on that is to murder not only Luis Navarro but perhaps the most compelling element of our Philadelphia project.

History, of course, is how we tell it. George Lippard, who was faced with a period more violent than ours, was fond of this maxim. But he kept Penn alive for a reason: the founder actually tried to live up to his ideals. If the utopia was to be written, it would have to be practiced, too.

Shall we try again?

Lippard was born as the rapidly changing city explosively challenged Penn's ideals. By the 1820s, the Philadelphia port, some 100 miles from the Atlantic, could no longer compete with those of New York or Baltimore. In response, turning inward, Philadelphia merchants found markets for the city's goods in the South and built the railroads, to phenomenal profit, to get them there. But Southern trade put the city in alliance with the slave-holding South. This signaled a change. Riots against blacks and Catholics ensued, suggesting that Philadelphia was no longer interested in Penn's utopian experiment. Lippard responded by attempting to resurrect the founder's ideals.

The growth of industry made Philadelphia rich, triggering a new interest in history, heritage, and culture. Publishing, manufacturing, the arts, and science (why Thomas Eakins' *The Gross Clinic* is so important to the city's cultural memory) attracted thousands of immigrants every month. A renewed pluralistic Philadelphia flourished for all the skills it now possessed. Then, after the Centennial, when John Welsh installed "Toleration" above the Wissahickon, Penn's genius seemed restored.

But since 1910, when about one of four Philadelphians was foreign-born, Philadelphia has slowly, steadily, closed its doors. By 1980, Puerto Ricans aside, immigration had nearly stopped: then fewer than one in 15 Philadelphians had come from another nation. Our civilization, as any one that is effectively closed to the world, had withered; our greatest hope became the 76ers' Moses Malone.

Turning further inward, angrier and more desperate, in 1985 we took to bombing our own citizens. And yet, as if that MOVE explosion shook hard enough to bust the lock, just then folks began to come again. For the first time since 1910, the percentage of Philadelphians who are foreign-born began to increase, now to its highest level since 1950. They come from all over the world—Vietnam, Liberia, the Philippines, China, Mexico, Nigeria, Ukraine, Ethiopia.

Can they lead Philadelphia to Venetian splendor? On a November morning I set off to find out—by leaving. I cross the Ben Franklin Bridge to Camden. From there, using New Jersey's new light-rail train, the RiverLine, I head north along the Delaware, ultimately stopping in Riverside, a town now infamous for an intolerant stance on immigration. I find it a quiet place. There's a lone skateboarder on Pulaski Avenue, on the west side opposite the tracks. His wheels scratching macadam make the only human noise. Otherwise birds. Otherwise the rustle of leaves and dried corn stalks tied up for a now-passed Halloween. It's a densely built but commodious town. There are sidewalks. And I am the only one using them.

At the center of town, an American eagle sits atop a brass globe and below that are the names of boys the town lost in the First World War. What strikes me is that so many of them are ethnic names, perhaps the same names of soldiers the other side lost: Luzio, Oblizinski, Vessinio, Cucinotta, Cohen, Acquaviva. There are American flags everywhere. It's a while until I find the Brazilian colors, words in Portuguese, traces of the 4,000 or so who settled here from impoverished northern Brazil in the past handful of years. Their appearance in the town was sudden and forceful. Brazilians transformed the place. Then native Riversiders, feeling as if their town had been stolen, struck back. The town passed but never enforced and then retracted a law making it illegal to rent an apartment or provide a job to an illegal immigrant.

But the damage was done.

"It's a problem," says a man wearing a kitchen apron outside of the churrascaria (steak house) on Scott Street. Many of the other immigrant-owned stores and restaurants have closed. "The people are going for Philadelphia," he continues. "Just a few are left here."

"Will you go, too?"

He looks at me and smiles. His teeth are yellow, gums swollen. "Maybe," he says.

I take the RiverLine south, cross the bridge, switch to the elevated line to Frankford, and head back up the other side. In Frankford, I get off the train and walk. The plane trees and turrets of Oxford Avenue carry me up to Oxford Circle and onto Castor Avenue. I see my first Brazilian flag at Higbee Street, a few blocks up. Then near Levick, a poetry of the immigrant street: Tropicana, O Boticario, Welcome to Brazil, Little Brazil, Best of Brazil.

Some estimate the population of Brazilian immigrants along Castor Avenue to be as high as 15,000. Brazilians flee Riverside for Castor Avenue because they feel safe here; in fact, Portuguese is only one of many languages spoken in the neighborhood, where Indians, Pakistanis, Koreans, Africans, and Albanians have also settled in recent years, a polyglot that for sheer diversity takes the attention away from any one group. So Brazilians, like most of Philadelphia's immigrant groups, seem to fly under the radar.

Yet as Washington continues an aimless assault on immigration, including a change just that week making it harder for even naturalized Americans to gain employment, Philadelphia will have to decide just how much to defer to the man with the high hat. Many cities, seeking to protect and welcome immigrants, have declared themselves sanctuaries.

Sanctuary cities don't make immigration status a condition of law enforcement or the provision of services. Officially, Philadelphia isn't one.

Should it be? Some pro-immigrant advocates think it's a critical answer to nativist activism like Riverside's. I asked Pedro Rodriguez, executive director of Action Alliance of Senior Citizens, and a veteran activist, what the city should do. Rodriquez, who speaks with equal vigor and good humor about Hollywood stars, literature, and Marxism, is a well-studied leftist born in the Dominican Republic. He came to Philadelphia in the 1980s, the last time the city considered becoming a sanctuary, agreeing to shelter the Salvadoran and Guatemalan victims of civil war. Then, to justify the position, city officials cited Penn's principles and Philadelphia's 19th-century role in the Underground Railroad. "It makes sense given who we are," he says.

Are immigrants aware that they, like the rest of us, are the inheritors of Penn's utopian experiment? Perhaps they come for a broad sense of American tolerance, but many wish only to survive, save for the future, and send money home. But to Philadelphia, they represent a kind of spiritual, but also physical, renewal. And so on Castor Avenue, as on Snyder, on Chester, on Passyunk, they bring energy, opportunity, ideas—enough to fuel the brilliant urban evolution, in a sense to mimic the adaptive genius of Venice.

But, as Mumford explains, Venice was a totalitarian state. Its political order was "based on an ultimately demoralizing combination of violence and secrecy....This system must have hampered every variety of honest work, candid judgment, and trustful collaboration, causing those at the center to be stultified ... by their own morbid fantasies and collaborations." Here, indeed, to greater and lesser degrees, is what has been since the 1970s (with a respite during the Rendell years) the strange state of the Philadelphia political machine.

To therefore allow Philadelphia to evolve by means of immigration—as all American cities must—will require that either the machine co-opts new immigrant groups or that the city installs a new sense of openness. Perhaps that openness needn't be a utopian one. One wouldn't call New York a utopia. But unlike New York, Philadelphia isn't primarily a commercial city; instead it survives as a city of personal relationships buffered by ideas. Those ideas—the most compelling, anyway—are Penn's utopian beliefs in tolerance, friendship, and love.

Nevertheless, some who help set immigration policy, including the leaders of a key pro-immigrant center, believe discussing sanctuary status for immigrants isn't really an effective sign of openness. Rather it is a red herring, a distraction from the real work of integrating newcomers into the region's economy. They fear that merely bringing the issue to light will result in an anti-immigrant backlash in Harrisburg. "From our point of view there is no [need for a] public conversation," insists the head of one group; instead it will be more effective to work underground.

But Rodriguez counters that Philadelphia—that city of ideas—is uniquely positioned to "challenge this limited view." He argues that "we have to be able to publicly express" and clarify what is today a murky position. "Philadelphia has everything to gain and nothing to lose," he concludes. "There is no need to hide our position." And, he adds, "Philly's grown up." He means that it's a more satisfying combination of Venice and Utopia than it has been in his time here. To clarify, he mentions a recent night at the Brazilian restaurant Picanha, at Castor Avenue and

Hellerman Street. "It was packed," full of all kinds of people, he says. A woman sitting near his table thought the restaurant had a liquor license. She hadn't brought wine. No matter, a group of men sitting nearby were happy to share. To Rodriguez, the simple act of friendship and good feeling was something new, a direct consequence of an open posture. Philadelphia seemed that night like the kind of city it declares itself to be. "It's never been like this before," he says.

CHAPTER 2

Living in Ruins

ABOUT 100 MILES UPRIVER FROM PHILADELPHIA, and especially in the Delaware Water Gap National Recreation Area, the territory is replete with the remains of an agricultural people—and before that scattered civilizations of Lenape and European farmers, trappers, hunters, and traders. A favorite path on the New Jersey side of the river is the Old Mine Road. Part macadam, dirt, and gravel, it winds along the river past withering stone walls like some kind of Anatolian highway. Here bergamot and wild carrot, loosestrife, thistle, phlox, yellow flax, and the outrageous common mullein (with its yellow flower tower) are having a field day in the fallow pasture. The farmsteads, barns, porches, outhouses, and the stone walls that once demarcated property are left to the will of the autumn olive trees, the bears and vultures, the deer and pheasant.

The trees untreated, gypsy moth caterpillars devour whole stands of forest—in the summer of 2007, 170,000 acres of woods in Sussex County, New Jersey alone—evoking an overpowering sense of lost control. The moths themselves drift along the roadside. Spotted touch-me-nots grow in every crease where mortar has disintegrated. "The spotted blossom hangs like a pendent jewel," says *Peterson's Guide*, "succulent stems exude juice when broken." Blacktop breaks away, as does roof slate and the red paint of the barns. Enter one of those empty, putrid-smelling barns: the flapping of wings, the slight sound of movement, your heart might jump for all the marvelous waste. Just to get in there to dig around the loose boards means bushwhacking wild flowers, bulrushes, reedgrass a mile high, drifting through a panoply of butterflies, legs bitten and shredded by the angry, defensive thicket. At the stone trestle of a washed-out bridge, an American goldfinch darts past bunches of joe-pye weed to gain ground in the tops of the fireflowers of the sumac trees.

Downstream in Philadelphia meanwhile, in gracious ceremony and with the aid of symbolic water from the Nile, officials close the archeology dig at the President's House at 6th and Market. The house, where both Washington and Adams lived as President, was demolished in 1832; the corner is part of Independence Mall, the sacred public space that extends north of Independence Hall to the National Constitution Center. But until 2002, the sacrament ignored the issue of original sin: there was no mention in the entire Independence National Historic Park of slavery. A local historian reminded the public that slaves were kept in the house and that the actual slave quarters were to be covered by the entrance to the new Liberty Bell Center. The irony proved too much; the Liberty Bell Center was pulled back from the site and an archeological dig ensued, at once reifying the space and putting it to question.

The dig, which helped illuminate the stories of the slaves kept there and which unearthed, among other finds, the architectural detail of the bow window (the bow was part of an addition to the house ordered by Washington), perhaps adapted at the White House in Washington, D.C., was to so many Katrina-like in its power to expose our nation's—our city's—original sin. There are apparently enough Americans who felt shame in the staining of George Washington's reputation (and would rather such a big deal wasn't made about his indiscretion) that it's vital to tell the story of slavery there. Now, indeed, in the slaves Hercules and Oney Judge, we have gained new national heroes, and made our first one, Washington, into someone more powerfully complex.

For us Philadelphians, the excavation is also a way to explore another kind of loss. While Washington lived here, Philadelphia began to build a permanent presidential mansion. But Washington worked behind the scenes to move the capital to Virginia, which the nation did in 1800, a year after his death. Of all of Philadelphia's losses, this was the most devastating. The artifacts of all this, in particular that evocative bow window, were lying all those years hidden right beneath our feet.

On the day the President's House dig was ceremoniously ended, I biked with my children to a favorite spot of ours near the Delaware Water Gap. It too is a little ruin, of a bridge washed out by a hurricane in the 1980s. And in summer it is lush. The road leading to the bridge is overgrown; in tall meadows bears and vultures take turns playing. On trips there we're often greeted by a partially eaten corpse of a deer and, in spring and summer, by butterflies and birdsong. On this day, as Philadelphia resanctifies one of its most powerful ruins, just at the edge of the road before the creek, we find a dead rat. We cover the rat with stones from the bank of the Flatbrook. Returning a couple of days later, I pull away the stones: there is nothing, or so little I had to search for the few identifiable bones, a bit of skin, a single claw. It's as if the creature hadn't ever existed.

Now too at 6th and Market there is nothing. The traces of Washington, of Oney Judge and Hercules, have been removed. But unlike the rat we buried at the edge of the Flatbrook, what was excavated at the President's House won't go away; indeed we'll live with it as a memory, as the ideas and artifacts inside the museum that will be built there, as the disputed and uneven ground on which we stand.

These urban ruins are our inheritance. We grapple with them as we do William Penn's utopian ideals; they are for us a burden and that burden can cause us grief and pain. Old buildings, as old ideas, often feel like they're in the way. Sometimes, we try to bury them—an act that is painful and terrifying. What if what we build instead is no better? What if it too falls down at our feet?

In his memoir *Istanbul*, the Turkish novelist Orhan Pamuk describes the city of his childhood and the overpowering sense of loss, a collective "melancholy of the ruins," produced by a century and a half of decline that marked the sunset of the Ottoman Empire. The melancholy itself he calls in Turkish *hüzün*, "the black mood shared by millions of people together."

"*Hüzün*," he concludes, "does not just paralyze the inhabitants of Istanbul; it also gives them poetic license to be paralyzed." Philadelphia, to certain observers, often feels similarly content with its own squalor and decay. "How do they live this way?" is not an unusual reaction by outsiders, often New Yorkers, who can't imagine a populace so docile they'll put up with such precipitous neglect. "Corrupt and content" is the way early 20th-century journalist Lincoln Steffens famously described Philadelphians.

There is, to be sure, a Philadelphia paralysis, the result of more than a half-century of decline and 200 years' accumulated loss. In some neighborhoods this translates as fear of outsiders and a related incapacity to imagine the place improving. Nothing new, the adage goes, could possibly be any good. The writer Thomas Keels says that living amidst loss, most especially of special places of a remembered architecture, has produced in

Philadelphia from time to time a kind of civic grief. On the 1952 demolition of Broad Street Station, Keels says:

> Even though an agreement to demolish Broad Street Station had been in place since 1925, the destruction of the building (postponed by the Depression and World War II) took countless Philadelphians by surprise, much like the death of an elderly but vital aunt whom one had assumed would live forever. Philadelphians' sorrow transcended the loss of a familiar, lifelong locale, the scene of countless memorable meetings, arrivals, and departures.

The grief is steepened, as has been the case so often recently, when buildings of historic merit are demolished without care, without a planned replacement, or without the kind of public review that the streetscape of an old and important city would seem to merit. This was the case at Front and Chestnut Streets in Old City, where a developer without a plan demolished two of the city's last remaining early 19th-century mercantile buildings.

In such a case, grief begins to feel like fiery pain. What are we doing? we ask helplessly. Why are we doing this? No good answer comes, only the wrecking ball and a bunch of hardhats with a job to do. We look on transfixed by the ease of it and then, on this particular corner anyway, something sparks, what was the center of the open, trading city of the early 19th century goes up in flames. The fire crew brings a 50-foot-tall shower head that pours 80 pounds per inch of Delaware River water onto the smoldering remains, and calms the flames, and quiets the dust. By then two traffic cops are spooning themselves "cookies and cream" ice cream from pretend Chinese food containers, and the buildings are down by three stories, leaving the best parts of the corner, the Palladian window arches and the Mexican yellow paint on the stone pediments, if only for one more cool night of the spectacular spring. The police officers eating ice cream remind me of a photograph of the Denmark Bookstore in London during World War II. The store has been bombed; it is open to the sky from the first floor. Debris covers the floor; floor beams from above hang down like ladders to book stacks that no longer exist. Three men in overcoats and hats stand before the bookshelves. They are browsing, reading, scanning titles. They might as well be eating ice cream.

Do we feel anything beyond helpless grief? Perhaps there is a Godlike power in the destruction, or merely the power in knowing life goes on. There is rage and power in the destruction. In that case it's a joyful act, a release, a way to condemn our ancestors for not being good enough. These were, after all, a pair of plain, four-story buildings, essentially unadorned, built to manufacture money. Never very special. Used up and out of time.

As Keels explains in *Forgotten Philadelphia*, our grief is often enough met by faith—born perhaps of American optimism—in contemporary ideas powered by an imperative to move forward. So thinking proudly, we might interpret the demolition of the maritime buildings at Front and Chestnut as faith in our own ideas and vision for the city. While the water rained down and the restaurateurs along Chestnut mingled, smiling in the serene air, the trades were busy finishing two large new condominium buildings nearby, at 101 Walnut Street and 22 South Front Street. The fire was out and the firefighters were putting away their armaments when the hardhats up the block hit the head and went on home. Standing in the middle of Front Street, I wondered if they had been watching the demolition, if from the 60-foot perch of glass and steel they noted the thickness of the brick walls, the heft of the joists—all of it now just a pile of rubble down below. Did they think about the buildings they were then constructing? Did they begin to wonder how long these buildings would stand before the wrecking ball came?

In other parts of the city, where only demolition crews appear, decline feels merely hopeless, breeding fatalism and desperation, reflected back and forth between people and their crumbling streets. "The *Istanbullus* of my era," notes Pamuk, "have shunned the vibrant reds, greens, and oranges of their rich, proud ancestors; to foreign visitors, it looks as if they have done so deliberately, to make a moral point. They have not—but there is in their dense gloom a suggestion of modesty. This is how you dress in a black-and-white city, they seem to be saying; this is how you grieve for a city that has been in decline for a hundred and fifty years."

To be sure, the ruins of this city define and circumscribe our ambition. Sometimes, as the President's House ruin was to the National Park Service, which initially opposed the dig, they are real obstacles. They won't allow Philadelphia to be Los Angeles or Tokyo or even Washington, D.C. But perhaps quite differently than in Istanbul, they do provoke us Philadelphians to dream; and in so doing they become the raw material of our inventions.

The intersection of Kensington Avenue and Somerset Street in Kensington, a stop on the Frankford Elevated, is something like one of Istanbul's "poor, outlying neighborhoods" explored by Pamuk's "lonely writers." This is the city's top drug corner. A half-dozen blocks up, the corner of Kensington and Allegheny bustles; two El stops south, Norris Square feels gentrification coming. But here at Somerset, there is nothing more ambitious than the massive ruins of the Orinoka upholstery mill. (The five-story mill complex made wool, cotton, and silk until the 1930s, when that work was sent to the South. Mill operations dwindled then finally ended in the 1990s.) Heroin, following the script of decline, is at present the neighborhood's most prodigious commodity.

On a black day in January, like hovering vultures, men drift around the El station's two stairways. They are young, groomed, missing teeth. They wear tattoos. They are addicts and dealers, fiercely alert and disconnected all at once.

I try to pass unnoticed. But, as I step down from the station, I'm spotted by someone who is younger than his mottled, gloomy face suggests. He watches me cross north on Somerset Street, and catches up while I wait for the light to change. "What time you have?" he asks.

He doesn't want to know the time, but I tell him anyway. "Around 11:30."

He nods and I look at him. We're standing on the corner. "Watch out," he says, assuming I've come to buy heroin. "Cops are laying out behind those buildings."

Across Kensington Avenue, past still more addicts, runners, dealers, a handful of men pushing handtrucks, the voices are loud and the conversation is animated. I follow two men in their twenties. "Dude, you got to do it now. Now's the time. *Right now*," says one.

"OK, dude, OK. Now's the time," replies the other. "I'll do it. Dude, I gotta do it. I'm doing it, I'm going to detox tomorrow." Methadone clinics occupy old rowhouses, fire stations, health clinics. Addicts drift in and out of them; they are veterans, laborers, secretaries, college students. Junkies sense cops everywhere. They squat in vacant buildings, shoot up when they can. They get clean needles and other supplies—cookers and choy—from the mobile needle exchange. They buy methadone on the street.

But on this January afternoon, it begins to feel like only heroin can pierce the darkness. That's until I notice a sign, a few doors beyond the dealers. "Relax . . . Play Darts," it says in a script of another time. This is Widdy Dart Boards, the workshop that supplies serious American dart players. The store wasn't anachronistic in 1935.

Joe Marafino, an affable man with a round face and pleasant smile, inherited the business from his father-in-law, Charles Wittmeier. Marafino makes by hand the 2,000 wooden dart cabinets that Widdy sells each year ($75 each), most of them to customers on the East Coast. Upstairs, his wife makes the darts. I ask him if business is good. "It gets harder every year," he answers. But you're still here, I say hopefully. "Where you gonna go?" he shrugs.

Caridad Delgado, the persuasive owner of Pio Pio, the Cuban restaurant three doors closer to the El, has an answer. "I thought about opening in other places," she explains, "but there I'll never own. *This is mine.*" Here then is the conceit of the newcomer, which sees opportunity and beauty even when locals see only death and decline. Though her ambition is circumscribed by the dimensions of her building, by the age of its systems, by the layout of its floors, and by the state of this corner in general, we might say that Delgado is like those who demolish old buildings to build new, who, in Keels' parlance, make a blow for "a bright new world." It may be that this attitude, and the sheer power of the newcomer's vision, is why here in Philadelphia, unlike perhaps Istanbul, civic grief doesn't always end in paralysis.

I sit at the white tile counter at the front of the restaurant between the wide case of pastries and the espresso machine. Pio Pio is a bright place with peach-colored walls and framed photos of Cuba. Delgado's sister Ydalma, who's just emigrated from Havana, serves me a fried pork chop, rice and beans, the $5 lunch special, so much food I need the espresso just to digest it. While I'm sitting there, their mother arrives, then a few Cuban regulars for café con leche. Soon the front room has filled and the jokes are flying.

Delgado, who immigrated seven years ago, is that kind of *dueña* who is capable of doing several things at once. Her confidence infuses the restaurant. She doesn't have a lot of Cuban customers, she says (there aren't many Cubans in Philadelphia), but overall business is growing. "Give me a couple of years. They'll find me," she says with enough bare bravado to scare away a dozen dealers. But Delgado knows she's on someone else's territory. The corner is controlled by drug dealers, some of whom, according to local officials, own the buildings along Kensington Avenue. They keep people busy, money flowing. In effect, they—and Marafino—manage Charles Wittmeier's ruins. Widdy darts remain popular, in part because they recall for people what is remembered as a special time.

A photograph of the neighborhood taken from the El tracks once would have shown dozens of mills, their smokestacks firing, their looms turning. Though a good many of those mills have been demolished, others remain. Some, like Orinoka, stand, rotting, valueless. The jobs they offered were never replaced. This may be why there are quite possibly more addicts in Kensington than anywhere else in the city, and some of them are prostitutes. Nearly everyone is poor. They are themselves a kind of ruins, of a social neighborhood of intimate ties, long gone.

Pamuk tells us that,

> to "discover" the city's soul in its ruins, to see these ruins as expressing the city's essence, you must travel down a long labyrinthine path strewn with historical accidents. To savor Istanbul's back streets, to appreciate the vines and trees that endow its ruins with accidental grace, you must first, and foremost, be a stranger to them. A crumbling wall, a wooden tekke—condemned, abandoned, and now fallen into neglect—a fountain from whose faucets no water pours, a workshop in which nothing has been produced for eighty years...a row of houses with crooked window casings—these things don't look beautiful to the people who live among them.

And so while Marafino shrugs and waits out his time, while junkies hover and cops lie out, Delgado sees hope and opportunity. She dreams.

In Philadelphia as in Istanbul, the outsider carries the power to see and imagine—and therefore transform. "If I can pick [Kensington] up," she says excitedly, "I will." But the key to her proclamation is the first word, "if." It implies there is a necessity of the ruins. The necessity says you can't simply do what you want. You can't turn Somerset Station into Sunset Boulevard. Not overnight, not ever. One must instead adapt—if it means offering rubbery American donuts instead of *pasteles de guayaba*—and negotiate if she is to survive.

Some of the most charming and beautiful parts of Philadelphia are actually in places like Kensington—and the Northern Liberties, Germantown, and Frankford—where the grid relents and streets, back alleys, and avenues are free to amble unburdened by Penn's orderly grid. Philadelphia is a million of those charming, intimate spaces, all those interiors of blocks and hemmed-in corners, and special renovations with stone and stucco and bright colors. As in Pamuk's Istanbul, these places entice us the most. Unlike in Istanbul—Pamuk explains that members of his generation prefer not to restore the old wooden houses—they are the kind of ruins we are drawn to the most.

Between 3rd and 5th Streets in the Northern Liberties, it feels just a little like a lost world: amidst the dozens of wildly disparate and somewhat overblown new rowhouses, morning glories climb signposts and cats dart and late-season begonias—their leaves parched and therefore the color of sea glass, their flowers drained to barely pink and yellow speckled—linger on, insistent and therefore ravishing. Giant paulownia leaves are underfoot. They've landed on a patch of luminescent blue brick paving, that strange bejeweled cobblestone found also in the factory ruins of Kensington. Out beyond are weeds, frogs perhaps, and the rusting carcass of a Citroën.

In Frankford, among streets named Mulberry, Meadow, and Plum, a family of woodworkers—brothers Ian and Matt Pappajohn and their crew—are gathered around a broad wooden table in the shade of an elm tree, eating takeout Chinese. In lissome air, among carefully restored buildings (one, of stone, that dates to the 18th century), one is greeted by a ruins transformed. This mill, where Jacquard looms were made for a century or more, is now home to cabinetmakers, designers, architects, and a coffee-bean roaster.

Like the traditional ruins of a lost civilization, this one is also a monument—to the idea that what is hard and harsh and ugly might someday seem beautiful. That possibility, of seeing beauty in ugliness, and the act of polishing the found jewel pushes us on. Parts of Germantown, in the northwest of Philadelphia, are being saved this way, its lovely ornamental finials scraped and repainted, its garden walls and ornamental iron fences (those that haven't been stolen) repaired and painted. The streets are as lovely and authentic as Montmartre. There, a lady who makes violin bows inside a handsome storefront on Germantown Avenue, shows off the oldest schoolhouse in the city, with its thick stone walls and shutters recalling a Norman tavern. All of this sits across from a gabled, rambling, exuberant Flemish composition (with a new life as condos and stores), seemingly lifted from the Grote Markt in Haarlem. Pamuk tells us why "many *Istanbullus* do not like seeing old wooden mansions restored: When the blackened, rotten wood disappears under bright paint that makes them look as they did at the height of the city's glory and prosperity in the eighteenth century, [*Istanbullus'*] lovely degenerative connection with the past is severed." Some Philadelphians, it turns out, have no such phobias. Instead, living in ruins—restoring, reconfiguring, adapting—is an embrace, another act of love.

But the ultimate impact of this embrace is limited in part by a significant and telling mismatch between the form of the city that grew rapidly in the 19th century—the height of Philadelphia's industrial and scientific glory—and the rhythms of contemporary life. That city was a collection of districts connected by busy commercial avenues, where Philadelphians worked, shopped, and sought entertainment. There are probably 15 of these avenues, which on paper probably connect half the city's population in one way or another. As life-patterns shifted, the avenues lost their purpose. Today they are chopped up, abandoned, and repulsive—and to a great degree empty, too. There are blocks after blocks—40 perhaps on Germantown Avenue alone—of remains, a solid city skeleton with bones left dangling, useless.

The trouble is, in a world of many Wal-Marts, we aren't sure what the avenues can, or should, be. Built on a more muscular scale, they're symbolic of the ambition of the big city. Without them, Philadelphia reverts to a premodern collection of districts connected only by the El above. And down below, the streetscape tends to drift. Buildings come and go. Hulking ruins, like the old Orinoka mill, deteriorate. They too feel useless, but they also seem to taunt us. "You'll never be great again, Philadelphia," say the ruins. At times this seems unbearable, a pain amplified by addicts and prostitutes who camp there, making the whole neighborhood feel like a netherworld of rot and ruin. Then, as it so often does, a fire breaks out. Eventually, all that's left is dirt charged with relief, tinged by hopelessness.

At Kensington and Allegheny, the intersection of two avenues and one El stop from Somerset, an early summer fire turned a vacant warehouse into an inferno. A few months later, but for melted vinyl siding across the street, it's hard to see evidence of the fire. The lot where the warehouse once stood is cleared and graded. Reflecting the late summer sun, it's a beacon of light from a place that was dark indeed (neighbors say it was a "shooting gallery," where addicts squatted, took drugs, and set fires).

Now life continues—bored women stoop-sitting, mopping their steps; children running; workers standing in line for empanadas at El Coqui at F Street; mothers awaiting their young ones outside the Ascension Church's school. The church itself, constructed at the turn of the last century, towers over this neighborhood of two-story rowhouses with bay windows, contiguous porches, ample flies, and the faint sound of construction now endemic to our streets.

"There was a sound like tzzzzzz," says a neighbor, John Calloway. Calloway has a soft voice and no fierceness—or fear—in his eyes, as well as a diamond stud in each ear. "And then boom! The transformer blew. See all these porches? They glowed orange. I'll tell you what—when the wind shifted, I thought it was going to be like MOVE."

One of the busiest neighborhood El stops, Kensington and Allegheny (known as K&A) boasts scale, worthy architecture, wide sidewalks, and a vitality that barely endures beyond drug dealing and prostitution. The neighborhood around the intersection is densely populated and growing, by 6 percent from 1990 to 2000, when the Latino population increased by 984 percent. Here, neighbors speak 26 languages, including Persian, French Creole, and Vietnamese. About a decade ago, a tall, 22-year-old fire-breathing circus performer with long hair and dreadlocks named Shane Claiborne came to K&A, took over a sprawling corner house, and began listening to and helping neighbors. Claiborne is a sort of Christian hippie who emulates the asceticism and love of early Christianity. "We came here to be good neighbors," he says. He launched an organization, The Simple Way, which bought several buildings and started a community garden, a few businesses, and an after-school program. The fire, which leveled much of H Street beyond the warehouse, destroyed several of The Simple Way's buildings and put an end to some of its programs, but the group organized the recovery, raising money, boarding up houses, and providing counseling for families who'd lost their homes.

At the corner of Potter and H, thanks to the fire, there is bright sand and gravel instead of buildings. Claiborne—that visionary outsider—sees a community center and a park. "I took a neighborhood kid, his head in my hands, and we turned to face the lot. I said, 'What do you see?' He said, 'An empty lot.' I repeated my question until he got it. 'I see trees.' His eyes finally lit up. 'A place to play.'" But city officials don't seem to have any particular plans, no sense of what K&A could be, no budget to build. Rumors of possibilities drift around, but no one but Claiborne and his companions believe. We might call this maddening disconnect the melancholy of the ruins.

CHAPTER 3

The Elevated City

IT'S FITTING THAT IN 2007, THE YEAR MICHAEL NUTTER was elected Mayor of Philadelphia, Pantheon brought out the 50th anniversary edition of *The Leopard* by Giuseppe di Lampedusa. Lampedusa's wise and tender novel—the story of the fading Sicilian aristocracy—makes great use of the parched island. Sicilians appear as recalcitrant as the soil itself. "Sleep, my dear Chevalley, sleep, that is what Sicilians want," says the book's protagonist, Fabrizio Corbèra, Prince of Salina (played by Burt Lancaster in Visconti's 1963 epic film adaptation of the novel), to a bureaucrat from the north who has come to try to convince the prince that he should join in the politics of the just-emerging nation of Italy. "They will always hate anyone who tries to wake them, even in order to bring them the most wonderful of gifts."

Lampedusa is describing a kind of melancholy of the ruins, of course—"these monuments, even, of the past, magnificent yet incomprehensible"—the psychological toll of 25 centuries of outside rule and nothing produced of their own, generation after generation conditioned to having no control, and gaining no benefit. Likewise in some Philadelphia neighborhoods, inhabited too by people of what Lampedusa calls "terrifying insularity," residents can't conceive it possible that a developer or City Hall or even a fire-blowing prophet would bring something of benefit to their streets. So it isn't surprising that a boy standing at the corner of Potter and H would need careful prodding just to imagine that something as simple as a playground might come from an empty lot. Had Shane Claiborne asked an adult to visualize the corner, the answer surely would have been "nothing good." After all, what, besides rudimentary improvements to the El station itself—or the new Dunkin' Donuts with its orange and purple flags spread across the parking lot—has been built there to make it better? By campaigning for more, Claiborne unwittingly may be raising expectations—dangerous business in a place that hasn't received anything of merit in years. That's why, says Don Fabrizio, "in Sicily it doesn't matter whether things are done well or done badly; the sin which we Sicilians never forgive is simply that of 'doing' at all." It sounds just like the Philadelphia that former *Inquirer* columnist Steve Lopez describes in his 1998 book, *Land of Giants: Where No Good Deed Goes Unpunished*.

Nutter's candidacy for mayor was predicated on the hope that this sort of somnolence might end, that our old and tired city could be shaken awake, its political discourse and polity elevated. If Philadelphia wasn't quite suffering a mid-19th-century Sicilian backwardness—"the well-known time lag of a century in our artistic and cultural life"—it was mired nevertheless in an opaque political culture of deal-making, corruption, and machine control. As a candidate, Nutter offered something quite different than the usual platter of municipal gifts. Instead he would deliver a strategic, forward-looking, culture-changing platform of openness, investment, and high standards. His was an attempt to seize on gains in openness and professionalism made by Ed Rendell, now Governor of Pennsylvania, who was elected mayor in 1991, and on the subsequent embrace of a reform candidate, the businessman Sam Katz, who lost the race for mayor in 1999 and 2003. Philadelphians almost miraculously accepted Nutter's offer; upon becoming mayor, he said of the city's troubles, "I've had enough and I'm not taking it anymore."

"We are located right between the financial capital and the center of government," he said in his inaugural address. Here Nutter takes the usual source of civic grief, removes two centuries of regret, and turns it into strategic advantage. His goal is, in effect, an unburdening. Lift the melancholic, incapacitating weight; allow our expectations to rise. No longer would a boy stand before an empty lot without imagining the prospect of a possible city.

But no mayor—no matter how persuasive, inspiring, and willful, no matter his skills at forming alliances, no matter how insistently he aims his ambition, no matter the expertise and grand vision of his deputies—can so easily remove a conditioned, and defensive, and ultimately incapacitating pride. Lampedusa, in the voice of Don Fabrizio, explains the extent of the delusion:

> The Sicilians never want to improve for the simple reason that they think themselves perfect; their vanity is stronger than their misery; every invasion by outsiders, whether so by origin or, if Sicilian, by independence of spirit, upsets their illusion of achieved perfection, risks disturbing their satisfying waiting for nothing; having been trampled on by a dozen different peoples, they consider they have an imperial past which gives them a right to a grand funeral.

Nutter responds to it with characteristic directness. "We need to get over ourselves," he says on the day after the election. If only it should be so easy.

The illusion of perfection is no greater in Philadelphia than it is in Rittenhouse Square, where a kind of imperial pride in a precious urbanism translates into an attempt to control behavior. This was the case in the spring of 2007 when police, at the request of certain caretakers of the park, began to enforce an obscure law against "musical presentation or amplified sound."

That is, you were no longer allowed to play music (or sing) in the park. The noise, apparently, was disturbing neighbors.

This is, indeed, ironic. Rowhouse streets trap and amplify sound, so Philadelphia's physiology makes it uniquely susceptible to uncivilized behavior: when properties are left to decline and trash is tossed out a car window, when snow and ice are left unshoveled, when car alarms and revving motorcycles and gunfire ring through the night, everyone on the block suffers. This city turns quickly downcast and miserable. You want to—but can't—assert some control.

But Rittenhouse Square is different. Philadelphia's most urbane place of grand and metropolitan scale, its busiest and most cherished public space, the Square at its best functions above the fray of private meddling and is therefore open to all, at all times. Jane Jacobs calls the constant activity "a ballet," and then quotes a local resident at length:

> First, a few early-bird walkers who live beside the park take brisk strolls. They are shortly joined, and followed, by residents who cross the park on their way to work out of the district. Next come people from outside the district, crossing the park on the way to work within the neighborhood. Soon after these people have left the square the errand-goers start to come through, many of them lingering, and in mid-morning mothers and small children come in, along with an increasing number of shoppers. Before noon, the mothers and children leave, but the square's population continues to grow because of employees on their lunch hour and also because of people coming from elsewhere to lunch at the art club and the other restaurants around. In the afternoon mothers and

children turn up again, the shoppers and errand-goers linger longer, and school children eventually add themselves in. In the later afternoon the mothers have left but the homeward-bound workers come through—first those leaving the neighborhood, and then those returning to it. Some of those linger. From then on into the evening the square gets many young people on dates, some who are dining out nearby, some who live nearby, some who seem to come just because of the nice combination of liveliness and leisure. All through the day, there is a sprinkling of old people with time on their hands, some people who are indigent, and various unidentified idlers.

Add to this half-century-old description the presence of artists and musicians, Frisbee-throwers and sun-bathers, and the Rittenhouse of today remains a "nice combination of liveliness and leisure," its brilliance achieved by that implicit sense of openness, an ease manufactured by diversity of interests and schedules.

In the open city, however, you can't bottle that "nice combination"; it's always changing. That's what makes it brilliant, enticing, elevating. But instead of letting the pervasive urbanity be, Philadelphia's defensive pride sometimes gets in the way. Some Rittenhouse caretakers begin to think that their jewel is so precious it needs extra protection. So they seek to control what should be left alone.

On a May afternoon, Drew Gillis, the rock/blues guitarist, looks out across the Rittenhouse fountain, past the children laughing and the strollers, past the guard house, past the lovers stretched out on the grass, past the ash and plane trees and magnolias whose leaves blow hard in the wind. He sees none of it. His eyes are clouded by pain.

Gillis, who grew up on 25th Street in Fairmount and plays in the band Stone Soup, is one of the targets of the Rittenhouse music ban. "All year I look forward to spending the summer here, playing guitar, teaching, exchanging ideas," he says and squints as if to bat away the apparent public ambivalence. Despite collecting 4,500 petition signatures against the music ban, he isn't sure that people really care.

After all, sometimes it's still possible to play music in the park. Ed, another regular park musician—who teaches young children and charms their mothers—has simply asked the guard, "OK if I play?"

OK as long as Wilkinson isn't the policeman on duty. If he is, it's not possible to ride a bike, throw a Frisbee, or play a viola. A citation will be given. For Drew Gillis and other regular musicians whom Wilkinson has already warned or cited, the punishment is likely to be worse. That's the result of power wielded arbitrarily, without just cause or reason. It makes no sense, as Gillis notes. Breakdancing circles, for example, are allowed. "Philadelphia wants to be a city of artists," he states, "and that's what we [Rittenhouse musicians] are; we learn from each other, play together—all the best musicians I play with I met playing in the park." They come from all walks of life.

"So why don't you play now," I ask. "Wilkinson isn't on duty."

"Then people will say everything's OK. But it isn't," he replies, lighting an American Spirit cigarette. Arbitrary power—bullying in this case—is stultifying; it destroys the essence of an open city, exposing that carefully honed illusion of urbanity. But for a moment Gillis begins to dream, "We can do things to make [the Square] nicer. Music is a stepping-stone." He mentions a nonprofit he's starting—PARC—the Philadelphia Artistic

Rights Council. PARC will advocate for public art, street performance, and the free exchange of ideas.

In *The Leopard*, the forward-looking bureaucrat Chevalley continues to press Don Fabrizio. He wants the prince to join the new senate as representative of Sicily ("for the progress of the country," he dreams), but Don Fabrizio won't relent. He sends Chevalley away thinking, "This state of things won't last; our lively new modern administration will change it all."

In Philadelphia, if not perhaps in Rome, a change in Rittenhouse Square doesn't have to wait for the new administration. By early summer, just after Nutter wins the critical Democratic primary, the police agree to back off. Wilkinson is transferred. It appears they've been influenced by the same desire to elevate the city beyond mere private interest that pushed Nutter convincingly past his more traditional political rivals. Philadelphia in one small measure has done what Nutter implores it to do: get over itself. Unburdened from overzealous hands, Rittenhouse Square returns at least momentarily to a lofty perch. Now again it feels democratic, entertaining, and beautiful—the ultimate crossroads in a city for everyone.

On a bright Tuesday afternoon in late January, the Northern Liberties is dusty—some combination of road salt, construction debris, crumbling infrastructure, and tailpipe emissions from the two highways that manage to keep the neighborhood feeling like a place apart. On Orianna Street I pass through the heavy metal door of an old auto body shop. This is the house of Scott Erdy and Dave McHenry, architects whose forceful and responsive work connects back to mid-century Modernism and forward to an expressive and flexible social architecture of the future. It is their willingness to push the geometry of building—of process, meaning, form, and function—that has made them desirable to clients who are trying to solve multiple problems at once. What Nutter has sought to elevate in public discourse, ambition, and expectation, Erdy-McHenry and other architects seek in the built form. It is no accident that these searches for elevation occur in rough parallel.

Inside the glass conference room below the firm's mezzanine library, Erdy, whose gentle face is covered by a three days' beard, and whose eyes are heavy from constant work, searches for images of the Radian, an apartment house they are building at 40th and Walnut, on the edge of the University of Pennsylvania campus. But he has found something else instead. "Here's something you're going to love," he says.

Projected on the screen is a stand-alone café with a glass terrace overlooking the Christ Church burial ground across 5th Street and otherwise attached to one of the intimate side gardens on the east side of Independence Mall, designed by the landscape architect Laurie Olin. An installation like this one is entirely unprecedented in Philadelphia, where a notion that public spaces should be kept pure from commerce leaves parks without the amenities and vibrancy they have in other cities. The café—"Open air, full throttle," says McHenry—is the kind of sensitive, surgical intervention that transforms public space. It's also a wonderful reminder of the tension in Philadelphia between Venice and Utopia. The original plan of the late 1940s and early 1950s for Independence Mall and Independence National Historic Park eliminated the amalgamated city—three full blocks north from Independence Hall and three to the east. Here, the evolution of this part of Philadelphia was stopped, reversed some 200 years, and frozen uncertainly in 1776. In 1957, Mumford called the maneuver false historicism. Venice was sacrificed for a very particular 18th-century utopia. Laurie Olin's redesign of the Mall, now completed, answers some of Mumford's critique of the empty Baroque approach to Independence Hall from the north; he wanted intimate, engaging conveyances that would encourage lingering. He gets them in these gardens, and in the café itself, a subtle injection of "now." The streetscape, no longer frozen, is alive again. Indeed, the large block-letter C-A-F-E etched on the long front glass wall readily proclaims its pedestrian purpose.

The café is a small project for Erdy-McHenry, but one which ably demonstrates their desire to make architecture that connects people to each other and to the city. A Drexel University dorm they are building emphasizes student interaction and shared space while responding to the constraints of the narrow site itself, a small plot next to the campus tennis courts on 34th Street. The 18-story building is really two half-spheres that rotate toward Center City, maximizing views and the building's presence.

Radian, the massive floating residence overlooking the western half of the University of Pennsylvania campus, has like a lot of the firm's work the quality of a viewing screen—or a wall of TVs, each a different size and tuned to a different channel. With a model of the building in front of us, McHenry is explaining to me why the building rotates (to create views and allow sunlight to penetrate Sansom Street), but he stops when I mention that this building seems to rise above a familiar Erdy-McHenry plinth. "Why do all your questions start with assumptions?" he wonders, betraying a frustration with observers—not just me, I imagine—who wish to pigeonhole the firm into a signature style.

McHenry's annoyance may be justified. Far from being an architecture driven by concept and style, the Erdy-McHenry approach is painstakingly responsive—to a project's site, its uses, context, views, street presence, and contemporary desires for control and environmental sustainability. To not understand that is to miss what is most important about contemporary architecture: the way it attempts to account for a democratic array of desires, users, and functions. Thus, Radian's plinth is meant to provide space for a street terrace with a green roof and retail stores; to connect the building to the distinctive block of rowhouses on Sansom Street behind and the campus superblock in front, to maximize sun exposure, street life, and social interaction, all on a mid-block site that's a bit small for the project's ambition.

The original architecture of Philadelphia—neat, unadorned, low-slung, and accessible—was a reaction to the sovereign, overdecorated, and vaunted cities of Europe. The result is an almost painfully intimate cityscape, sometimes oppressive in its insularity. Despite their normative approach, Erdy-McHenry's buildings similarly share a common but opposite reaction. Their buildings seek elevation. They seek sky, openness, views, and they are happy to turn—or stretch—to get them.

This is no easy task in Philadelphia. In fact, the options are slim, indeed. Most of the city is built at a scale 25 to 35 feet high—two and three stories—on blocks no more than 50 feet wide. Many observers have linked this airless form to a parochial worldview (that is, no view), and a politics reliant on personal relationships. That is an oversimplification. Philadelphia has long been, despite its built form, a city of ideas, of innovation, and reform. It is also, because of that form, a terrifically social city, and a comfortable place to live.

But the search for real air and openness (as opposed to governmental transparency) is an even stronger, more flagrant instinct. While politics seems to work in cycles—from machine to reform and back again—outside of Center City (whose skyscrapers have grown taller), there are fewer opportunities in the built environment to

elevate today than there were during the last period of political reform in the 1950s and '60s. Factories and mills and schools built to
look like factories and mills—and as sacred architecture, churches,
too—once filled the skyline. A substantial portion is gone. What's
been lost to the streetscape is not just scale, but an opportunity to get
higher. Those mills are famous for their windows, fire escapes, and
balconies—places from which working people could see past the
neighborhood to something beyond. Their continuing loss leaves
most Philadelphians with one consistent opportunity to see out,
that is along the route and in the stations of the Market-Frankford
Elevated. The views may never be spectacular, but given a chance to
amble across a station's chicken-wire-enclosed overpass (many stations have one entrance, requiring the riders going in one direction
to cross the tracks), with silvery tracks in the infinite depth of field,
and undulating brick, bridges, and even trees across the horizon, one
is treated. Up there, one gains a—or rather, many—perspectives.

This is doubly the case because the El is the fastest and
most efficient way to travel across the city, making
Philadelphia seem larger (for all the places it takes you) and
smaller (because it so easily connects otherwise disconnected
places). Scale is intrinsic, for the El travels 13 miles end to end
and provides 180,000 rides a day, half again as many riders as
the entire 10-route Regional Rail system, which covers about
425 route miles. The duality of scale and speed is a hallmark
of the large, infinite city. So it is probably no surprise that
Erdy-McHenry's work seems to confirm this theory, for each
of the firm's current city projects—a potential development at
46th and Market (which I once had helped to conceptualize),
the Radian, Drexel's two dorms, the 5th Street café, Hancock
Square (now in its second of three phases)—is located within a
couple of blocks of an El stop. From University City to

Fishtown and the Northern Liberties, their projects measure a city of elevated vision, ideas, and ambition.

It takes 15 minutes on the El to travel from the Radian at 40th Street to the firm's lauded Hancock Square at Girard Avenue. From Girard it is just two more minutes to Norris Square, a Kensington neighborhood with an eponymous park about the same size and scale as Rittenhouse (and indeed, with a church of historic character on the same northwest corner). The location of the churches aside, these are vastly dissimilar places; and yet at least some caretakers of both squares struggle to apprehend the lofty promise of an open city. In Rittenhouse Square, overseers from time to time seek behavioral control (at present, arm rests are being installed at the center of the park's benches to prevent a person from lying down); in Norris Square, certain leaders seek just the opposite: to be free of people who might not tolerate noise, poverty, and disarray. Despite the opposing instincts at play, leaders of both neighborhoods betray a similar defensive, parochial pride; their squares must be carefully protected from what they perceive to be the wrong kinds of outsiders.

On a warm afternoon in early February, I sit facing the playground in the center of Norris Square. The air is wet and the sky is dark and there are shouts: a crew of women collecting trash along Howard Street, a handful of boys playing basketball after school, a pair tossing a football, and the blast of a moped gunned at 30 miles an hour and heading this way. The air still seems to vibrate and the moped's already gone—the wrong way on Dauphin Street.

You can hear the El train, too, but just barely out of earshot is the Latin music that emanates from several Front Street stores below the tracks. It's rare to find a shopping district below the El that survives. But this one, now with its first *taquería*—Las Chivas at Jasper Street, which replaces a check-cashing joint—is colorful, loud, and stuffed with cheap clothing, toys, and housewares.

"It's a little dirty, grungy, *pero* what's been interesting about [Front Street] is it's always been packed with people," says Pat De Carlo, the executive director of the Norris Square Civic Association. We're sitting in her office—what was an ornate bedroom—on the third floor of the turn-of-the-century brownstone that had been Fluehr's funeral parlor. The square is just below.

De Carlo, who is in her sixties, has a full oval face and short white hair, and she speaks in long, trailing sentences peppered with Spanish. When I enter her office, she is on-line, reading about President Bush's proposed cuts to the Department of Health and Human Services. "I think poor communities are entitled to live in nice neighborhoods," she says. "It shouldn't be when they start fixing things up, people with money start calling the shots." So it is her self-described task to mend a neighborhood by keeping people with means away.

The effort to reclaim Norris Square began in the early 1980s when a bunch of young mothers, who had grown up playing in the park, grew tired of broken glass, drug dealers, and disarray. They formed a group that eventually became the Civic Association and the Norris Square Neighborhood Project, which has focused its resources on maintaining the Square while using urban horticulture to build community. The Neighborhood Project builds evocative Puerto Rican gardens and in partnership with Philadelphia's Mural Arts Program, paints brilliant Caribbean-colored murals on vacant lots north of the Square and provides after-school activities for children. De Carlo, a lawyer and organizer who served in the Peace Corps in Costa Rica, emerged from the early days of local Latino activism to run the *Cívica*.

She knows that the growth of the Northern Liberties and

Fishtown has brought her neighborhood into wider view. With two El stops, a large square, strong rowhouse blocks, a colorful shopping district, a handful of good-looking but abandoned textile mills, and a new public school on the long-abandoned site of a long-vacant state welfare office, Norris Square is the kind of place that excites an imaginative city planner.

De Carlo's group runs a day-care center, an after-school and community Beacon program (with skill-building and learning activities for adults and children), Head Start, GED and job placement, a violence reduction initiative, has built affordable housing (construction of a 48-unit townhouse development just below the El tracks is now under way), and ran El Mercado, the farmer's market at Front and Palmer that eventually failed (critics say it tried only to appeal to people from Puerto Rico). The Civic Association also owns several key parcels, including a monumental abandoned bank at Front and Norris, near the Berks El stop, the land across the way now designated for the Kensington Creative and Performing Arts High School, and the St. Boniface church and monastery on the south side of the square.

If land is power, then the Civic Association has it. That, in turn, means De Carlo's ideas for Norris Square have mattered most. But those ideas "don't jive with what Philadelphia wants to be—a multi-ethnic city," says Pedro Rodriquez, who lived in the neighborhood until recently (he left in frustration) and as a resident spent several years on the board of the Civic Association.

De Carlo deflects questions that imply her neighborhood has *the potential* to elevate. She says instead that it's a unique place because she has fought to preserve it as a Puerto Rican enclave. "Once people have struggled to do all these things, they shouldn't have to move," she says, fearful of precious and uptight yuppies demanding that neighbors pick up after their dogs or paint

their houses in certain pre-approved colors (or turn down the
music). "*Sabes*, how do you stem the tide? You like it here, you
want to come eat in our restaurants, buy up our stores, go for it.
You want to come live here? No."

De Carlo talks joyfully about a period she spent as a farmer in
Puerto Rico. "It was a grand ole time," she says of the farm where
there was no electricity or running water. Her belief in self-suf-
ficiency—the village model—seems to stem from this experience.
In De Carlo's model, the city is a collection of parochial districts
joined by the elevated train. The center—Rittenhouse Square,
say—is open territory. But everywhere else is closed but to day-
trippers. Hop on the El, get off in Chinatown, black 52nd Street,
Italian-American South Philly (after switching to the Broad
Street Subway), or Norris Square. Each neighborhood is free to
protect its own heritage—and with well-defined boundaries is un-
threatened by the others. The districts can be insular, if they so
choose, or, as De Carlo suggests, welcoming to tourists from the
other districts. In this she is struck by the success Chinatown has
had maintaining its identity. "How many times have the powers
that be tried to move those people out?" she asks.

But far from a one-note village, Chinatown is the commercial
center of a richly diverse, pan-Asian community that isn't just
for immigrant Chinese or Chinese-Americans. With cultural
and economic connections to people throughout the city and
the region, and with a housing stock that suits a wide range of
people, it feels as unashamedly open as Rittenhouse Square and
the place seems as vital as ever.

A neighborhood need not be closed in the ways De Carlo
imagines in order to protect a cultural heritage. Indeed, it's
ridiculous to think it might. Culture is as fluid—over time and
place—as are neighborhood borders. Heritage, so often a source

of identity and pride, is a beguiling concept, especially when placed in the urban context, where by definition so many people are thrown together. Perhaps it's the great noise of pluralism that sends certain individuals off to seek a particular identity. Others, like De Carlo, may be struck by a kind of nostalgia for a certain historical moment—and the place where that moment was lived. This may be dangerous. "People say, 'You know, Pat, you can't discriminate,' but there is no protection for the neighborhood," says De Carlo. What she means is that she'd like the neighborhood to remain Puerto Rican—and poor—a utopia taken from a Caribbean farm and transplanted to a city neighborhood. "I understand it is hard what I propose," she continues, meaning the attempt to surgically regulate the neighborhood's development. "If we can figure out how to protect [the people here, we might] bring in [some, but] not more than 20 percent [artists and other outsiders]."

"At that rate it will take 300 years," says Rodriguez, who believes that as the neighborhood becomes more mixed, fewer people will stand for "Old World" tactics that amount to exclusion.

"What really makes me angry is that kind of mentality," says Victor Negrón, of De Carlo's narrow definition of "neighborhood." Negrón grew up in Norris Square and recently returned. But he became quickly frustrated by the Civic Association's lack of responsiveness to residents. In response, he formed the Friends of Norris Square. "Not to compete" with the Civic Association, he cautions, but because "we want to build community, not look at [people's] tax records."

Like the city itself, heritage isn't static. Rather it's always evolving. The beauty of Mumford's Venice comes in the evolution; the downfall of Utopia is its rigidity, meaning that it is unable to account for the movement of time (De Carlo's Norris Square can no more remain Puerto Rican and poor than More's Utopia would remain a nation of 24 equal cities, or William Penn's town a Quaker city). Negrón, who is the marketing director for a large health care corporation, says, "You're allowed to not want gentrification. I'm Puerto Rican and I wish the neighborhood was more Latino. But you can't control the market."

Indeed, as a Latino enclave, Norris Square is changing. One resident, a Latina visual artist who lives in a brownstone facing the square, says of De Carlo, "She speaks of Puerto Ricans but in fact many here are Dominicans and the Mexican population is growing." As in many neighborhoods, this means that through negotiation and assimilation, a new culture emerges.

And yet in a neighborhood replete with evocative gardens that mimic the Puerto Rican rural ideal, it's hard to deny a different elevating power, that of vision and memory. "The past is a spiritual strength and not the literal, physical past," says the character in another Mediterranean novel of change and longing. This is Murtada al-Shamikh, the protagonist of Hassan Nasr's *Return to Dar al-Basha*. Murtada has returned to Tunis after a 40-year absence. The city—or what happened to him there as a child—pushed him away. People are always running from cities, so this isn't unusual. What may be unusual, however, is that in an act of self-discovery Murtada returns.

"What spirit are you talking about?" his cousin wants to know. Murtada hasn't an answer. But as he explores his old neighborhood—Dar al-Basha—he discovers the source of its inexplicable power. It returns to him a lost childhood. The trouble is, in Dar al-Basha as in Norris Square, the emergent, captivating power is based in memory and personal experience, which critically belies the city's need to elevate, to move forward; according to Nasr, it belies reality:

The conditions of the world and of nations, with all their different customs and their sects, do not persist according to a single fashion and in a constant form. There is, rather, a fluctuation over time and through different eras and a transition from one condition to another, whether for individual people, times, or major cities...This holds true for Dar al-Basha as well.

Broadly speaking, Pat De Carlo wishes to deny that fluctuation. At the very least, she hopes to avoid it. "Do me a favor," she asks, "don't call attention to us. That would be the worst thing you can do." She stops for a moment and then continues. "Sometimes I think, 'If only we didn't have a square.'" It's a desperate prayer fit for one of Don Fabrizio's monologues. The Sicilians, he might say, would trade the beauty and strategic location of their island for a chance to be left alone, to control, at long last, their own destiny.

But a neighborhood with two El stops really can't hide. De Carlo's conceit is therefore plainly destructive. It can't survive the city that seeks light and openness. But can residents be made to feel that development might enrich their lives? "The intention is good, Chevalley, but it comes too late," is Don Fabrizio's reply, when he is told Sicily will benefit from being part of the new Italy. For Michael Nutter, the Philadelphia mayor, it is not too late. Rather the question emerges right at the beginning of his term; set to project his high-minded vision out across the vast city, across the hundred Norris Squares, to convince the hundred Pat De Carlos, he cannot now know how it will be answered.

CHAPTER 4

Estuary of Dreams

To get to Lubinville from my part of town, it's easiest to transfer to the 33 bus. The 33, which carries about 17,000 passengers each weekday, traverses the length of Center City before crossing the Benjamin Franklin Parkway and heading into North Philadelphia, all the way to the edge of Nicetown. Mid-morning northbound makes this powerhouse of a people-hauler a lonely carriage. The driver shimmies the bus cheek-to-jowl with another going opposite. He opens the door to shout salutations to the other driver. Their voices are sweeter than Butterscotch Krimpets.

Snow covers some streets and the widening expanse of vacant ground. Now the bus stumbles across Girard Avenue into un-plowed territory. Outside, as the bus creeps north, we pass furnished rooms to let (handmade signs saying so) and deranged Venetian blinds exposed to the wind. Roofless bay windows are open to the brilliant sky.

Newly constructed tract houses with driveways appear on desolate blocks in groups of four or eight. The 19th-century scribe George Lippard would say the houses are shivering, miserable, suicidal. I tell myself they are the last asthmatic gasp of the social engineers. I am the only one on the 33 who cries. The bristling religious poet Stephen Berg, whose Mt. Vernon Street house is served by the 33, captures the dreamlike despair of this bus, what so often feels like an irreconcilable convergence of possible cities. It is a painful clash. Berg gives it breath:

> Stitches have popped and unravel, the coat collar of the
> woman sitting beneath me on the aisle is coming apart, her

shoulder bumps my thigh, her dense black rag of a wig is spray-sheened, each earring a tin snake hoop swallowing its tail, the spotty fake gold-dip plating, once buffed bright to help them sell, all but gone now. Her face is a blank. My face—I can feel the moral part of me choosing it—has a smile on, a forced poise in this atmosphere of poor and black and What can be done? What can I do? I don't look hard at anyone, I don't hate, I don't want to be on a bus whose heat works, or is clean; I follow the buildings as we pass, inhaling Woolworth perfume, mothballs, musty wool. Frost sweats on the window corners. A kid at the back hunches over, cups his hands between his legs. Sweet whiffs of grass. We careen by the Museum of Natural History, tipped into each other, standing, seated, scowling because we touch. The humped, tapering dinosaur profile fills the Museum's front window, as always, its back fins wide gray spikes of shadow. When I got home today a police car was nosed up onto the sidewalk, Millie and Margot were getting out. A cop was helping. Someone on the 33 had tried to tear my father's gold watch off Millie's wrist; he kept trying to pull it off, jamming his fingers under the strap in front of everyone, as if the bus were empty. He wanted what he saw and couldn't break the strap and Millie had to identify him at the precinct, file a complaint, then testify. Last night I heard her say, for the first time since I've known her, "I'm afraid, hold me." A whisper, a childlike, low cry. "I woke up, seeing the man again...on the bus."

Above Norris Street now, old friends, a man and a woman in their forties, catch up on babies, extra pounds, grown children, a cousin released from jail. *"You think he gets it?"* she wonders.

"There's nothing like freedom." Then a knowing silence emerges between them, the violence, shootings, life during the scourge of the gun, incomprehensible. Finally, she goes on. *"I just get up, go to work, go to the grocery store, come home and go to sleep. I don't even have time, anyway."*

Not far from the Church of the Advocate, we turn left then right to cross the Glenwood Avenue tracks. Then 22nd Street greets us with people, their shadows shortening as the day grows, rows of rowhouses and porches, silk flowers. At Lehigh the bus reaches the plinth once exalted by Shibe Park, and the scale shifts.

Here was the 19th-century city lunging headlong into the 20th. Here was baseball as popular entertainment for a city that was one-quarter foreign-born. Here, just across the tracks, was the world's largest radio factory, Atwater Kent. Here, in 1909, alongside Connie Mack, came an optician and peddler Lubin— the first to dream of the shadows of the silver screen. Bald and blind in one eye, Siegmund Lubin was Philadelphia's Faust. He was the maker of the Cineograph, perfecter of film stock, the vertically integrated maven ("World's Largest!") who made more popular films than any early filmmaker. He cheated Edison, saved Samuel Goldwyn and Cecil B. DeMille's careers, built the most advanced equipment, and recreated famous events on his roof. He opened the Auditorium, Palace, Savoy, and Victoria and made the Quaker City into Hollywood, which was the most incredible feat of all.

Philadelphia was his open studio. In Fairmount Park he staged the Spanish-American War, on Broad Street the American Revolution, in Chinatown the Corbett-Fitzsimmons boxing match (which had actually been contested in Carson City, Nevada). Never mind history. Lubin sold you his dreams—along with the projection equipment (for as little as $70 in 1897).

Until he opened his theaters—the original was in West Philadelphia in 1899—the first movie screens were the long walls of rowhouse living rooms.

Now I stand in front of Lubinville, where directors would make five motion pictures at one time. The sun is making puddles of the snow. The sky is periwinkle, the ground is bare and rocky. Matching the scene in front of me to the parcel maps of the time, I guess that despite the fire of 1914 the main studio building still stands, without the massive glass curtain walls and roof.

From the exterior Lubinville resembles any factory, wrote film industry observers at the time, until inside, beneath the glass ceiling, you found yourself standing beside a Hessian soldier or a headdressed Indian. Then you had to watch out or be placed under the spell of the wizard. He might cast you as a plantation owner. Or a fugitive slave. Or a belly dancer.

But Magic Man's gone. His empire collapsed in 1916, the year he made 128 films. Here in the earliest, still winterlike spring, I stand before the factory of dreams in the unsettling silence of a neighborhood called Swampoodle, amid rowhouses with iron balconies and porches covered by Astroturf guarded by concrete lions once painted white. Like many of Philadelphia's neighborhoods, this one only seems to stumble ahead into darkness.

Is it still possible to imagine the race of technology, the nervous confusion, the chatter of the beehive? In 1915, early film writer Esther Pennington said the studio's energy "has done more to arouse Philadelphia from its Rip Van Winkle existence than all the jibes of New York and Chicago. No one in Philadelphia knew the real significance of the Liberty Bell until a troupe of players in revolutionary colonial costumes rushed past the intersection of Chestnut and Broad streets, pursued by a man waving a camera." For three decades Lubin turned Philadelphians into his goofy fantasies. And those Philadelphians, in turn, consumed them. Perhaps they believed. The period that followed was marked by civic ambition. Expectations were raised. Philadelphia would turn its industrial wealth into cultural treasure. Ambitious city planning, including the planning and design of the Benjamin Franklin Parkway—interestingly as a kind of Parisian stage set—followed.

Perhaps we still believe. Philadelphia, without revolution, industry, or influence, lives on by invention. We turn to our dreams and project them—unevenly, haphazardly—onto the street. But in a pluralistic city, whose dreams should prevail? Whose should we pay most attention to? Should ownership of land matter foremost? The University of Pennsylvania, the city's largest private employer and most ambitious institution, controls a great deal of land along the west bank of the Schuylkill River. What the university does there, which matters to everyone, isn't open to public debate. In some cases, however, the dreams and ideas of neighbors might matter most. Community leaders like Pat De Carlo want control over their neighborhood's future (and they get it the same way the university does, by purchasing real estate); residents want to decide what buildings look like, how they're built, and what they're made out of.

And what of newcomers, those of independent spirit like Lubin? Some of Philadelphia's most successful, persuasive, and energetic citizens are those who transplant dreams from elsewhere, who find in Philadelphia's streetscape a chance to profit and grow. For others, like Shane Claiborne, Philadelphia's need reveals a calling. Yet a fundamental characteristic of the city's defensive pride is the dismissing of the ideas of outsiders—immigrants, transplants, hipsters, even politicians—who, it is imagined, haven't paid their dues. For this instinct to protect "the achieved perfection," thousands of dreams are postponed, transferred, and lost altogether.

In a city that survives on dreams, perhaps a better question is, should it matter who is dreaming so long as the dreams produce that elevated vision? The difficulty is removing the passion of ownership: leave the dreams but take away the dreamers. It sounds like heartless policy. But what happens when there are clashing dreams? At times, the clash produces energy—either defensive or proactive, or both—and an ensuing effort to implement the dream. Other times, as the poet Berg experiences while riding the 33, the collision produces an intractable melancholy. How then should we respond to each other?

The brilliance of Lewis Mumford's medieval Venice is the way its streetscape articulates some seven centuries of accumulated dreams. Its "splendor and order" were "merely the best that a succession of energetic merchants and industrialists, who courted money and power, and the luxuries that money and power can buy, were able to conceive." The irony, clear to anyone who visits Venice today, is that this process of amalgamating dreams has ended. Or, more precisely, the city survives as the Venice in the dreams of tourists, who wish not for a real city, but one frozen in a single—and imagined—romantic time. Thus, what is most important about city dreaming may be that the process remains alive and democratic, an enduring cacophony.

Leaving Lubinville, I walk east now on Lehigh Avenue, under the trestle, below the old tobacco factory, beyond the smoke towers and carved pediments. The dream metaphor nags at me. Yes, Philadelphia is the result of many dreams overlapping at once.

Some who dream big have the backing to build what they see in their minds. And so certain places are booming. But here in Swampoodle? There are dreams aplenty, God knows, but as far as I can see, there is no wizard, no projector, and the walls themselves are crumbling.

I head down the Byzantine temporary stairs of the subway. It's good to see the old North Philadelphia Station getting a facelift, but I know it's only a surface repair. This is the barely used transit hub of North Philadelphia: seven commuter train lines join here, plus the Broad Street Subway and Amtrak—a tangle of jet-black spider's legs on the map—converge in a sprawling and inscrutable multi-station complex. The renovation provokes a hope: Might something good emerge from this convergence? Might some able leader see the possibilities? There's a recorded voice on the subway now that tells the stops, the connecting routes. It isn't the radio disc jockey Michaela Majoun, whose comforting voice announces the stops on the RiverLink, rather some woman with a genteel British accent. We're to believe, I suppose, that Buckingham Palace is just overhead? The London Bridge? The Thames? This strikes me as a bad dream, a terrible fantasy meant only to deceive—and not to inspire.

There is another city (not London) along a river a hundred miles or so inland from the ocean. At times grand and ambitious—it has been a trading center for centuries—the city boasts a growing skyline. It is a large and bustling place but has been careful to preserve its traditional streetscape, too—ancient architecture, and a neighborhood-based culture. It has one famous university but is renowned as a center for medicine. Nevertheless, it lives right in the shadow of another city, this one a world capital of culture and finance.

In the last decade and a half of the 18th century, Philadelphia merchant shipmen found this city indispensable in establishing trade independent from Britain. They also found its waters eerily familiar, for the path in from the sea then up the river to the city's port appeared identical to that of the voyage through the Delaware estuary and up the tidal river to Philadelphia. They delighted in this doppelgänger, so much so that trade with this city soared, bringing sought-after items like porcelain, tea, and silk, and making the Quaker City rich.

Guangzhou, the energetic city on the Pearl River, is this double. The city once known as Canton is a provincial capital pushing ten million people that lies in the shadow of Hong Kong. The improbable duplication of form was mere coincidence, of course, but it gave Philadelphia firms and financiers a sense that they controlled the nascent trade and all the global connections it implied. In fact, Robert Morris, along with Daniel Parker of New York, sent the first American ship, *Empress of China*, to Guangzhou and by 1800, 40 Philadelphia-owned and based ships worked the China trade exclusively.

This early predominance in trade with China made Philadelphia the largest city in the New World. In his essay, "The Athens of America," the historian Edgar Richardson says that the China trade not only brought Chinese goods to America (much of which were already available through the East India Company), but access to the ancient, wealthy culture of the East. Trade builds relationships and as such it is the basis of a cosmopolitan city. It was therefore vital to the early rise of Philadelphia as the rich, cultured, elegant, technologically advanced, and global city that was given the name "Athens of America."

There have been a handful of attempts, including "world trade" and "free trade" schemes and zones, to reestablish

Philadelphia's predominance in trade. As of the late 1950s, Philadelphia's port handled 45 million metric tons of goods, much of it export; today the port (not including Camden and Gloucester City, across the Delaware in New Jersey) moves 5.3 million metric tons, most of that import. The folks who manage the Philadelphia port, however, are ambitious dreamers who believe Philadelphia offers advantages over other ports (intermodal connections in particular). They actively seek business, a tenacity that is beginning to pay off with extensive South American and now Mediterranean shipments. Philadelphia is the largest importer of Chilean and other South American fruit and receives cocoa beans, clementines, paper products, and meat and other food from the South Pacific. Lines to Europe have opened; others to the Far East are being planned.

This growth is fuel for the port's dreamers, who presently wish to expand the Packer Avenue Marine Terminal—a project called South Port—into the environmentally sensitive eastern portion of the Philadelphia Naval Yard. Implicit in the port's plans is the proposed deepening of the river channel to 45 feet, which will allow larger ships to pass. Although the shipping channel is now regularly dredged to maintain a 40-foot depth, a project of this size—the churning up of toxic compounds that now lie dormant—will cause at least short-term damage to certain fish and shellfish and bird species, and possibly threaten water supplies. Both ideas—the building of South Port and dredging to deepen the channel—place maritime shipping dreams directly in confrontation with others, notably those that envision the Delaware as a place for recreation and leisure.

At the Packer Avenue Marine Terminal, the shoreline is abuzz. The Walt Whitman Bridge swells above, but here the river is everything. Longshoremen, some of whom receive good pay and union benefits, are moving steel from the gray *Elena Topic* onto the flatbeds of trucks; other pieces go onto CSX freight cars. Meanwhile hundreds of containers sitting aboard the *Cap Sunion*—probably frozen meat from Australia and New Zealand— await the crane. Seen at short distance, these cranes are the majestic architecture of contemporary industry. They are powerful, the strongest one capable of lifting 385 tons.

Dredging has its rightful detractors, but political support for it and the port's expansion ($300 million committed by the governor) is symbolic of the city's desire to participate in and profit from world trade. While few expect trade to make Philadelphia rich, as it did in the 18th century, it isn't surprising that a city would attempt to exploit its natural resources and physical infrastructure for profit; indeed, it may be a sign of progress that the city is willing to project its strengths so confidently.

As the historian Steven Conn explains, the clearest upside of deindustrialization is a cleaner environment (he says that in the 1940s, with the city at its peak industrial output, the river died). Philadelphia's waterways, particularly, have since recovered beyond expectations. Fish and waterfowl species, including the locally feted shad, which had disappeared completely, have returned. Consequently, the Delaware is as healthy now as it has been in 50 years. A local foundation is considering the possibility of opening it, and the Schuylkill River, to swimming.

Might it be possible to capture some of the intimate magic of the upper Delaware? There, and most especially in the Delaware Water Gap National Recreation Area, the river cuts a fertile valley through sandstone and quartz. The protected river is dappled by hidden little beaches, buzzing cutouts at the edge of the woods rimmed by smooth cordgrass and tidal mud, access to which is gained by shimmying down thorny bluffs or following

trails of trampled brush. Like many people, I take great joy, three
seasons of the year, in swimming there. In spring especially, the
river's edge buzzes. Tadpoles form thick schools, and chartreuse
dragonflies sun on the sand. The only voices come from the oc-
casional passing kayak. In a dry spring the current is easy, and
the water forms the strong arms of a joyful hug.

Back downriver here in Philadelphia, behind the Wal-Mart
at Pier 70 (a mile from the Packer Avenue Marine Terminal), I
stand in front of a large, white sign half-covered in black graffiti.
"Danger—No Trespassing," it says. Just behind, in the parking
lot, the engines of a dozen idling tour buses rumble. Fifty-odd
others from New York and Maryland and Ohio—here tour op-
erators can park without being charged—jam the macadam.
Here is the origin of this city—Lenni Lenapes escorting the
Swede Sven Svenssen and his men up the shore, and later Peter
Stuyvesant and then William Penn, and still two centuries later
a tide of European immigrants a million strong—the powerful,
sealike expanse that has always inspired.

Remarkably, I'm not alone along this narrow stretch of grass
between the Wal-Mart parking lot and the chain-link blockade.
Chris, from Kensington, a man who appears to be in his fifties,
walks his two Shih Tzu dogs and draws on a pipe. He says he used
to take them to Penn Treaty Park along the Delaware in Fishtown,
"but Gizmo was attacked, so I don't trust the dogs there anymore." He comes here twice a day. Lovers lie on a sliver of grass
beneath a parking lot tree. Electricians on lunch break dangle
fishing lines—"Beats installing plasma TVs," says one—and here
geese bookend their gray goslings. The "Danger—No Trespassing"
is repeated a dozen times. The sun pours across our faces. We
stand gazing out, not at ease, not content, rather like prisoners at
the gate. There is hunger, but also sadness, in our eyes.

Curious, I roam the fence and in a few minutes come across an opening. Someone has bushwhacked a trail through lush mallow, sumac, and clover. The walk, which leads right down to decaying wooden piers, is a faint reminder of the wild upper river. But here a half-dozen hand-built cat shelters line the way. According to Chris, a woman named Linda comes every night to feed the hundred or so cats that live in the brush, put water in their bowls, and leave them plastic toys. She does this in defiance of Wal-Mart management. Chris says he doesn't understand their opposition. "They keep away the rats," he says, smiling.

So why dredge now? Why take waterfront land that's healthy enough to support a nesting eagle and use it for industry? Why deny us the opportunity to live out such a powerful dream as that which draws us, irrationally, it seems, to even the narrowest and most roughly defended stretch of shoreline. We want our river back.

But why deny the legitimacy of either dream? A bustling port is no less commanding than the alluring natural river. Indeed, it sends one's imagination into action. What if Philadelphia was a trading city again? What if it sought and attained vast commercial partners, and endless contracts; wouldn't we speak of— and without irony or sadness—a new Athens of America? Mumford would suggest we have a look again at the Venice of long ago. There, multiple—and conflicting—dreams were each given credence in a system of rational planning that segmented the city by use and craft, and later on, for leisure. This is how that rapturous city has always, even today as a simulacrum, supported heavy industry. Perhaps, then, we might better organize the uses along the Delaware. Port operations are scattered along three and a half miles of shoreline, intermixed with other industrial uses, public space, and retail. A Venetian-inspired plan, according to Mumford, would organize uses of the river so that one doesn't interfere with the other. With this as a guiding principle, a plan might consolidate port operations to the south, around the Packer Avenue Marine Terminal, and pleasure uses to the north, where abandoned former industrial land might be accessed to create a system of parks and swimming holes.

Early 19th-century Philadelphia produced little to trade on the world market. Philadelphia shippers were forced to triangulate trade—that is, to find a third party—so that when they arrived in Canton, they would have something to exchange for tea and silks. Shippers like Mordecai Lewis and James Large Mifflin made stops through Europe, the Mediterranean, and the Pacific, where they traded for things the Chinese desired: hides and furs—nearly making sea otters and seals extinct—sandalwood, tin, and opium. They also made themselves and their city rich; they gave it standing (and, indeed, made it known as the most cosmopolitan place in the New World).

As ships today leave Philadelphia empty, contemporary shippers are also forced to triangulate so that ocean voyages aren't wasted. The difference today is that ships don't originate here. Profits don't return. Philadelphia's just another well-positioned spot on the East Coast. A lot of people—consumers of Australian meat and Chilean fruit—live nearby. And yet we want shipping to signify more. The *city that was*—with a strategic global position—looms. As a dream it lingers. This, too, is part of our inheritance. Philadelphia isn't St. Louis, we insist. No, indeed. It has always wanted to be something more, and for a time last century, according to the historian Robert Caro, it seemed to have a role to bolster its global standing. In 1946, descending from the peak of its World War II-fueled industrial might, the city nearly made itself the ersatz capital of the world. Caro says that the commission chartered to find a location for a headquarters for the United Nations (the charter indicated the headquarters should be near New York City) was about to approve a site in Philadelphia (in far Roxborough, along the Schuylkill River). But John D. Rockefeller, Jr. intervened, providing the funds to purchase the land along the East River in Manhattan; by the earliest days of 1947, this latest dream, perhaps the last to forcefully project Philadelphia onto the world scene, was thwarted.

One imagines that had there been a more captivating and centrally located site, better connected to the symbolic power of Independence Hall, Philadelphia might have hung on (imagine then a very different elevated city). In the Philadelphia Naval Shipyard, we have that site now. The Navy Yard, which extends from the Packer Avenue Marine Terminal west to the confluence of the Delaware and Schuylkill rivers, is a two-mile-long stretch of waterfront, in total about the size of William Penn's original city. Decommissioned as a naval shipbuilding and maintenance facility in 1995, the Yard today remains a strange and wonderful place, dumbfounding in its scale of decay and sense of loneliness, electrifying in its possibility. A publicly funded arrangement attracted the commercial shipbuilder Kvaerner (now Aker) to the site. Aker builds merchant ships, using the Yard's dry docks, the largest in the U.S., in the shadow of gray naval ships still docked there. The city has also lured other private concerns—about a dozen major ones in all—most notably the retailer and merchandiser Urban Outfitters. That company has restored the marvelous ruins of brick and terracotta machine houses into a playful center for clothing and furniture design. A handful of suggestive admirals' bungalows remain and they are joined by a few lackluster new buildings, erected at the scale of a suburban office park. Beyond the central area, a ruins begins. Here, on fully half the site, a suburban village built for officers and enlisted men—with shops, recreation facilities, and little lawns—is given back to nature. As on the Old Mine Road, the macadam crumbles, meadow creeps; it's an eerie place adrift. But with all the water and sky, it's possible here to sense not isolation but connection—from this city through the lens of its historical position—to the rest of the globe. The scale, at the very least, is almost unimaginable: the height of the gray ships, bridges that span vast distances, the limitless mass of some buildings. It's also easy to fall in love with the adaptive reuse of the handsome brick and terracotta machine houses and with the dinghies and barges that rock and float on the little inlet nearby. It's a place of marvels, of disjuncture, of variety.

The architect Robert A.M. Stern was commissioned to develop a master plan for the Navy Yard. His plan contains solid and handsome ideas: bold connections to the waterfront, provision for a marina, the mixing of uses, including residential and recreation, the preservation of historic buildings (the firm says there are 187 of them), and enough office space to accommodate a corporate anchor. Stern would protect wetland, create parkland, and follow guidelines for green buildings and sustainable design. Altogether it makes an adequate design, but it lacks a compelling and unifying vision to match the scale, the pull of history, the site's position at the elbow of the wide, compelling river. According to Bennur Koksuz, who heads up the City Planning Commission's urban design unit, the city's vision for the Yard keeps changing—from suburban office park to cosmopolitan district. This ambivalence may be why the Stern plan seems uninspiring.

Philadelphia's particular magic may lie precisely in the way—as a ruins, as an underdog, as a place of intimacy—it allows its admirers to dream. It's in the combination of what it isn't and what it was that emerges what might be. Should it already be Utopia, one needn't improve it. What's more, there's enough land and raw potential, here at the Navy Yard particularly, to keep one up all night moving pieces around the ersatz chessboard. But where are the royal jewels to exchange for the porcelain and silk? Perhaps not as far as you might think.

Urban Outfitters employs hundreds of creative people to design clothing, art, and furniture; those bright young people mine the globe for ideas, which they translate and then transform into fashion. Value is added at every step of the way. Philadelphia doesn't have many Urban Outfitters, but it does have—across the region—82 colleges and universities. "Education is our business," says Mayor Nutter, and he is right. Education and medical institutions are the backbone of the Philadelphia economy. All those students and faculty—their research, innovations, ideas, books, and intellectual pursuits—are our currency. And every one of those institutions is seeking ways to connect more profoundly with the rest of the world, noticeably China and east Asia, where until a few years ago there was little exchange: Japanese and Chinese students came to America to study, bringing expertise back home. Presently, Philadelphia institutions in all disciplines—from the Beasley Law School at Temple University to Arcadia University's Center for Education Abroad—are forging vast connections with Chinese universities and polytechnical institutes.

These nascent relationships (which extend beyond China to the Middle East, South America, and Europe) are being forged department by department, one fact-finding trip at a time. But taken together they represent one of the most compelling ways for Philadelphia to reassert itself as a center for global trade: the trade of ideas, information, discovery, and culture. If played right, Philadelphia can claim the physical presence of this trade: a single campus of several international universities in America. Here is the bold claim the Navy Yard demands.

My campus idea is drawn from what has been for a century and a half—from 19th-century missionaries to 20th-century cold warriors—an American inclination to project the nation's culture, educational pedagogy, and economy abroad. As such, American universities in locales such as Beirut, Paris, Istanbul, Athens, Bulgaria, London, Rome, Cairo, Sharjah and Dubai (in the United Arab Emirates), Palestine, Girne (in Cyprus), Central Asia, and Armenia provide English-language higher education to students around the world. A few of these—Paris and Cairo, especially—are first-rate institutions that attract highly qualified international students. Their campuses are vibrant global villages inside of vibrant cities, one reinforcing the other.

I'd like to imagine there are a handful of nations which, for reasons of politics and economics, want to reach a North American audience with their own equivalent of an American University. Conversely, they want to provide a formal entry for their citizens to study and live in the U.S.—in their native language. Why do they choose Philadelphia? The easy answer is the availability of land in proximity to the center. The new campus of the American University in Cairo, for example, is quite large—260 acres just outside the city center. A handful of these institutions altogether will require that much to start in Philadelphia. But the more compelling reason is this: with more institutions of higher education than nearly any other place in the U.S., Philadelphia has the brain power and reach of top scholars and scientists, students, and innovators. If education is the city's business, ideas are its currency. It is what we have to trade on.

I'd like to imagine still that with some prodding, local university presidents might be able to exploit ongoing international programs to add dynamism to the Navy Yard campus. An illustrative endeavor is Penn's Annenberg Center for Global Communication Studies, directed by Monroe Price. The center has programs in Britain, Hungary, and China, among other places, Philadelphia serving as the center of a constant flux of scholars, practitioners, and students. Multiply Price's center across dozens of university departments. What's produced is a web of international relationships centered in Philadelphia. Amalgamate those relationships and officials at Sun Yat-sen University in Guangzhou might want to establish a Chinese university base of operations in Philadelphia.

Imagine therefore a Philadelphia whose purpose, and strength, is to be open to the world. There's much to be gained by this exchange, not only culturally and intellectually, but also economically. Investment desires openness; it abhors parochialism. Thus, Spain, with its enormous Latino immigration, is booming, while ever-more parochial Italy is not. Now imagine a waterfront campus housing several international institutions that share facilities and pedagogic models (with each other and our own host institutions), programmatic space for the international initiatives of Philadelphia's colleges and universities, seminars, lectures, and all the output of a scholarly and cultural exchange.

Then, an idea in hand, let Stern—or, better, a more imaginative architect—invent a master plan. It can't merely be a plan, but rather a proclamation. Ours is still an estuary of dreams.

When I left Lubinville, I took the Broad Street Subway south to Center City. It was an 11-minute ride to City Hall. Another

12 minutes on and I would have arrived at the Navy Yard—had the subway itself reached that far. Instead, the line terminates a mile short, leaving this place of scale and ambition disconnected from the rest of the city. Fewer than 300 people take the special shuttle bus between Pattison Avenue, where the subway line terminates, and the Navy Yard each day, meaning nearly all of the 7,500 people who work there arrive by automobile. It's a fatal disconnection. And so any plan for the Navy Yard, as Stern's indeed does, must include the subway extension—to and ultimately through the site, up to the entrance of the port, and perhaps beyond, to other sites along the Delaware.

But the subway extension is also a dream, the kind of obvious one that makes a more social, attractive, and exuberant city seem not very far out of reach. There are so many others like it, many of them derived from the experience of other cities, where transit, public spaces, and city parks seem more vital, exciting, and fun. What is it with this place, we wonder, why don't we have that? But before the words have escaped our lips, the dreaming has started. It feels like an act we can't control.

"I have always dreamed there should be a Tivoli in Fairmount Park," says Farah Jimenez, a Fairmount Park commissioner and the director of Mount Airy USA, a community development corporation in the city's northwest. She's referring to the amusement and entertainment districts in Copenhagen and Stockholm.

Why is that? What is it about Philadelphia that conditions, over and over, the same kind of response? It goes back to the combination of what was and what isn't. What isn't is a city that feels energized by the world around it. It's just not open enough. And that lack of openness leaves it feeling all too often more lackadaisical, somber, and somnolent than it should be. What was, of course, are the physical ruins of a city that in its scale, ambition, and architecture mirror the world's greatest. So we can't help but see our city as being one of them. But Stockholm—despite the Swedish colors of the Philadelphia flag—it isn't.

And so we dream. A Tivoli in Fairmount Park? In 1876, feeling rich and proud, Philadelphia invited the world to celebrate the nation's Centennial. About 10 million people came. The 700-acre remains of the world's fair—formal gardens, monuments, a zoo, and a grand hall—form the core of the west part of Fairmount Park. But it's a disconnected core, an all-too-empty core, despite including an outdoor musical amphitheatre, the Mann Music Center. So the Fairmount Park Conservancy, a park advocacy group, has commissioned a plan to build upon the ruins, with the hope of erecting a fully cohesive entertainment district from the present disparate parts.

In 1871, just before the Centennial, Philadelphians were feeling ambitious enough to design and begin erecting the largest municipal building in the world, what was hoped would be the world's tallest structure, a vision amplified by sculpture, carvings, and symbolism. The world changed considerably by the time City Hall was completed in 1901. Laden with corruption already, it immediately appeared a relic of a premodern age, and ever since we've used it begrudgingly.

Presently, just as the Fairmount Park Conservancy hopes to build upon the tantalizing remains of the Centennial, a score of Philadelphians are saying of City Hall's history, "That hardly matters now." City Hall is the most brilliant thing we have. What we do with it today is an ample test of the city's contemporary ambition.

City Hall sits on the fifth of William Penn's five original squares, still considered Centre—or Penn—Square. It remains the center of three branches of municipal government. Inside are court records, deeds, courtrooms, the offices of the mayor and representatives of city council, the chambers of judges, grand halls, portraits, hundreds of sculptures and friezes, and a courtyard that looks like the inside of a palace but feels like a bus station. There's nowhere to sit.

Centre Square is the southeastern axis of the Benjamin Franklin Parkway, a Beaux Arts boulevard meant to mimic the passage between the Louvre and the Arc de Triomphe in Paris. At the northwest axis stands the Philadelphia Museum of Art. In between, at Logan Square, is a Philadelphia Place de la Concorde. The library and courthouse there replicate the Hôtel de Crillon and the building that houses the U.S. Embassy. But Paris, sadly, this is not. The vast plaza outside of City Hall, above and below ground, connecting to the city's most important transit hub, and facing the art museum, is empty. There are statues, lamps, and last year, even a public toilet.

And so we dream, of ice skating rinks and lawns and movie screens and café tables and jugglers and artists and sculpture competitions and mini-museums and cooking demonstrations and gardening workshops; we dream of ice cream stands and vendors' carts and lunchtime dining and wine bars and free speech zones; we dream, as Mayor Nutter has, of farm stands, of tables upon tables upon tables punctured by a giant sculptural *Philadelphia stoop*, where under the shade of a Franklinia tree it might be possible to dream away an afternoon. (Benjamin Franklin deserves a place here because it was his persistence at the French court that produced the money for the American Revolution, bankrupted the monarchy, causing the French Revolution, and ultimately putting the Tuilleries and the New Louvre, the buildings from which City Hall was derived, in the hands of the people.)

These City Hall visions join our other, endless Philadelphia dreams: of uncovering lost streams, of building green roofs, of recreating remembered homelands, of diagonal subway lines, of bike sharing, of skateboard parks, of museums for art and immigrants and food, of literary events, of movie theaters, of drawbridges, of promenades, of wild ruins left to rot, of 1,500-foot skyscrapers, of restored trolley cars, of restored railroad stations, of train lines long defunct, of public climbing walls, of marinas, of street performers, of ice cream stands, of balloon men, of championship parades, of clean streets, of the political and economic reality it will take to make the dreams reality.

CHAPTER 5

Inventing Philadelphia

"PLACES DON'T HAVE AN INTRINSIC WORTH," says the Tunisian Murtada in Nasr's *Return to Dar al-Basha*, still searching for family members to help him restore his grandfather's house in the medina. "We're the ones who assign them an appropriate value by the love we grant them, the work that we realize there, and the schemes that we devise. With our work—not with dreams—we can increase the value of Dar al-Basha."

Benjamin Franklin couldn't have said it more clearly, or more precisely described the present reality. In a suburban nation, it's sometimes hard to tell if anyone cares about cities. Certainly it doesn't seem that politicians and policy-makers at the federal level see our old cities as a problem worth fixing. But a great many Philadelphians do. And all their work defines, to the greatest unassailable degree, the life of this immensely creative city. I am speaking of the young woman who on Saturday mornings at the edge of Kensington hands out clean syringes and loving, non-judgmental smiles to junkies and who takes those who ask to the back of the mobile clinic for an AIDS test; of another young woman, recently married, who provides counseling and support to elderly people in their Nicetown homes with the hope that they'll stay there longer, stabilize the neighborhood, and stay out of the nursing home. I am speaking of the man who transformed the triangle formed by three intersecting streets into an urban garden where now patrons of a restaurant can sit and eat in the open air; of the hippie artist whose sprawling mosaics have turned a neighborhood's walls into a living gallery, a biography of people and their ideas; of the tenacious and brilliantly analytic technocrat who keeps an entire city department functioning during crisis; of the imaginative green thumbs who've turned old industrial land, abandoned lots, and empty fields into productive urban farms that supply local restaurants; of the pair of brothers and their partner who keep expanding, reinventing, and adapting their two neighborhood bars into centers of a swirling polity; of the carpenter who instead of working for his own profit teaches troubled kids in North Philadelphia how to build, and to the kids themselves who've renovated rowhouses all across the city; of the city attorney who comes home every night and removes the day's accumulated trash from his block in Passyunk Square; of the immigrants from the Mexican state of Puebla whose music stores, *abarrotes*, tamale carts, taquerías, leather shops, produce stalls, and the green-white-red Mexican flag they've woven into the long-standing green-white-red Italian heritage of South Philadelphia, and whose licuados have changed the way that district tastes; of the West Philadelphia neighbors who patrol the streets and alleys night after night; of the young architects who design and build their own buildings, which now dot Fishtown, Kensington, and the Northern Liberties; of the furious resident who stands up at a community meeting to demand a developer's accountability; of the muralists who teach white, African-American, Vietnamese, and Mexican-American children how to paint and reflect on their own experiences of community and isolation, all the while turning a wall overlooking a grim parking lot into a brilliantly colored allegory on human migration; of the video store impresario who took over a floundering film festival and made it one of the most engaging weeks of the year; of the stubborn women in Norris Square who refuse to be intimidated by drug dealers on their corners and who by their own fierceness and love watch over neighborhood children; of the writers, poets, historians, journalists, archivists, librarians, and musicians whose unvarying engagement with the ideas, stories, and culture of the city's past keeps Philadelphia's metaphysical spirit alive and relevant, and of the blacksmiths, carpenters, metalworkers, masons, and plasterers whose simultaneous reinvention of the city's physical heritage keeps the architectural visions of past centuries in our open view.

"Dreams are beautiful," says Murtada, "but work is even more beautiful." This process, of turning individual and communal dreams, desires, ideas, and interpretations into a tactile and material reality is no more powerful than when the work in question is also art. So many artists are dreamers, of course. They imagine something else, another way. Then they paint it, perform it, and build it. A great number of Philadelphia artists build things, literally reinventing the streetscape: public sculpture, bus shelters, bike racks, park benches, houses, courtyards and gardens, parks, bollards, gates, an alternate world. "Art is the center of the real world," proclaims the celebrated muralist Isaiah Zagar, "Philadelphia is the center of the art world."

Michael Taylor, a curator of modern art at the Philadelphia Museum of Art, says to understand this it's simply necessary to travel back to the early 1960s, around the time Zagar landed here. In 1961, Marcel Duchamp came to Philadelphia for a panel discussion at the Philadelphia Museum School of Art (now the University of the Arts) and said prophetically, "Where do we go from here? The great artist of tomorrow will go underground." The Philadelphia art scene since then, according to Taylor, has been that underground, the antithesis of his hometown, the market-driven London. And right now, it feels, as Willem de Kooning said of Duchamp, like a one-city art movement open to anyone.

Taylor, who has a bright, round face and greedy eyes, hung the Philadelphia version of the 2008 Frida Kahlo retrospective and organized the wildly successful 2005 Dalí retrospective. His exhibit on the American artist Bruce Nauman has been selected to represent the U.S. at the 2009 Venice Biennale, and he's now at work on the first U.S. retrospective of the Armenian Arshile Gorky. But one of the moving currents in Taylor's life is his friendship with the perspicacious painter Tom Chimes, whose anthology, Adventures in 'Pataphysics, he organized last year. It's easy to see why Taylor has befriended Chimes, who is 86 and lives on Washington Square. Both men revel in the connections—among artists, ideas, events, and eras—that swirl around, infect, and take meaning from Philadelphia.

"You see," says Chimes, smiling, "this is a very important place."

The two men meet regularly at Zeke's, the 5th Street diner, and on a day in February they are joined by his wife, the professor of art history Sarah Powers, and Claire Howard, Taylor's research assistant. Zeke's is filled, the usual lunchtime crowd of dilettantes, lawyers, and grandmothers. Chimes, who wears a red plaid shirt, navy knit tie (the kind with the square end), and V-neck sweater, speaks in a measured, nasal tone, one that is sweet, almost hallucinatory. He's having fun reciting a speech he had just given to the Hellenic University Society of Philadelphia. In his speech Chimes reminded the audience of the power ancient Greece once had over him. At age 13 and attending a Greek school on 57th Street in West Philadelphia, he noticed a frieze, which he later learned represented a scene from the Aeneid. Interpreting that frieze led him into the imagined world of Ulysses. The key notion in his speech—an idea that seems to penetrate his work—is that time is pliable. Or, as Chimes says, quoting the French intellectual Alfred Jarry, "we should be able to travel through all future and past instants successively . . . we shall see that the Past lies beyond the Future."

It may be that Jarry's philosophy is absurd; the one thing we do know is that in Philadelphia it's nearly impossible to get to the future without stepping through the past. This seems to go for artists, too. And since the city's founding, artists have come. Many have struggled, particularly in the 18th and 19th centuries, to make a living and attract notice. Other cities sometimes seemed more financially supportive and intellectually responsive to new ideas. Quite a few early American artists, even those who kept Philadelphia as a base, spent years at a time in Boston, Baltimore, Charleston, Savannah, and New York. In 1813, a group of promising and influential painters, including portraitists Rembrandt Peale and Thomas Sully, attempted to define the range and style of American art by forming a sketch club. But after a year or so, several, Peale included, gave up on the place and left. Just the same, since those early years, artists have sought ways—by erecting museums and galleries, staging exhibitions and concerts, opening schools, and producing art as public spectacle—to make Philadelphia more urbane, exciting, and interesting.

This work continues ferociously today. Do-it-yourself galleries, collectives, and social networks are producing an energy that is palpable in certain parts of the city. This capability to invent is why we often assign artists special powers to transform the city. If artists are powerfully avant-garde, then to get a sense of the ways Philadelphia is being reinvented, one needs to keep an eye on them. Just where are they taking us?

"The art story is the same as the city story," says Genevieve Coutroubis, the West Philadelphia photographer who runs the regional community arts program of the Center for Emerging Visual Artists (CFEVA). Coutroubis, who spends five or six weeks a year in Greece making luminous, scorching, black-and-white street photographs, says "New York is New York and L.A. is L.A." But "it's hard to replace what we have," meaning the mixture of affordability, major institutions, art schools, art-making clubs, and support organizations that make it possible to "live as an artist and experiment."

"Philadelphia has always been affordable and a relatively easy place to live, so I'm very dismissive of re-saying this is a better time," says Jeff McMahon, a Philadelphia native and graduate of the School of the Art Institute of Chicago, whose cerebral and sometimes realist paintings explore the distance between artist and audience. McMahon, who wrote graffiti in El stations as a teenager, sees an art world ever more beholden to the wealthy and the life of the artist circumscribed by relatively few opportunities to break out. "It's like fucking playing the lottery, that's what an artist's life is like," he says, his voice deep and words deliberate.

Then he slowly corrects himself. "The artist's life is not a horrible thing, it's incredibly beautiful." The difference, he explains, is between the artist who strives to be a celebrity—"all artists want to break out, passionately, desperately"—and the art-maker, who loves to think, invent, produce. In this regard, Philadelphia artists are relatively lucky. Given the plethora of institutions, many work in regular jobs within the arts and academic sectors, jobs which pay enough and allow the flexibility to be productive art-makers. As the arts journalist Roberta Fallon, whose award-winning Art Blog chronicles much of the invention, puts it, "They live partially above and partially under ground." But in a global art market that embraces youth, style, and surface, and a local market that has relatively few commercial galleries, the difficulty in breaking through forces many to invent novel and not always financially rewarding ways—outside of gallery and museum—of connecting with an audience. Rembrandt Peale's frustration carries clear across two centuries. "We're always giving stuff away," says Fallon's blogging and art-making partner Libby Rosof about the paintings she and Fallon make.

As for the present versions of the 1813 sketch club, it's hard to tell if they too will dissolve in frustration. "It's entirely possible that do-it-yourself galleries won't last more than a year or two," says Fallon. "That's life," concludes Rosof. The larger point is that in Philadelphia artists are worth paying special attention to because they are establishing dynamic networks, pushing each other intellectually and artistically, buying one another's work, and, from Kensington to South Philadelphia, engaging in and transforming the life of Philadelphia's neighborhoods.

"Art is happening everywhere," says Coutroubis, whose organization supports artists within 90 miles of Philadelphia. "This is what is important about Philadelphia. Artists live and work in every inch of the city."

Perhaps more than most artists, Joseph Tiberino has embraced the easy play of the Philadelphia streetscape into his art and life. Tiberino is a living reflection of Mexican muralists like Diego Rivera and David Siqueiros and visionary Philadelphia art-makers and impresarios like Rembrandt Peale's father, Charles Willson Peale. His compound, which incorporates five houses and nine yards in Powelton Village, is as much like Frida Kahlo's Blue House as anything in Philadelphia might be. Tiberino's life combines art-making with celebration and social activism.

Steven Conn says that there have been only two family dynasties in American art and they were both Philadelphia families, the Peales and Wyeths (three if, including sculpture, you count the Calders). And then there are the Tiberinos. "The kids do what I do. They grew up with a mother and father doing artwork all the time," he says, speaking slowly with a Kensington accent. Peale named his sons Rubens, Rembrandt, Titian, and Raphaelle; Tiberino named his Leonardo, Raphael, and Gabriel. Raph and Gabe are working painters, as is their sister Ellen, named for their mother, the Pennsylvania Academy–trained figurative painter whose defiant art and life inspired the family's house-museum. Ellen Powell Tiberino suffered 14 years with cancer, ultimately, like Frida Kahlo, painting from bed. The courtyard—that assemblage of nine yards—is an undulating space filled with sculpture, a bar, a tree house, and found objects. Joe and Gabe's allegorical, figure-filled murals enclose the space. Near the entrance is a mural Tiberino painted about the MOVE bombing, which was deemed offensive to Mayor Goode and removed from Temple University, where it had been installed.

Sitting in the Tiberino house, it's impossible not to feel the presence of the Mexican muralists. There's an oversized *Mexican Mural Painting* tome on the shelf and a faded Mexican flag draped over a table and a small chapel with a painting of Ellen nursing Raphael in the center of the altar. "To tell you the truth, I never thought [Kahlo] was very good. [Rivera] was the one, you know," Tiberino says, smiling wryly. He wears a black-brimmed hat and thin gray beard and mustache; he stands close and grabs my arm for emphasis. Tiberino's work seems to combine Rivera and Siqueiros, the Mexican fabulist he adores most of all.

He takes me across the courtyard and into one of the houses that faces Spring Garden Street. There we pass his tragic-comic painting of Pope John Paul, Che Guevera, and Castro, and into a salon filled with his wife's paintings. The most captivating is clearly a charged piece, haunting and alive, a face in fiery pastels. Powell Tiberino made the picture from bed very near the end of her life. She had been in a coma for months; when she emerged she told her husband, "I've been on a long journey." "OK," he responded, "let's go home and you can paint it."

Now the painter grabs my arm; he's eager to show me his bedroom and studio, whose renovations are just being finished. The room is illuminated by midwinter's bright, diffuse light reflecting pure white walls and the calm of lima-bean green on the woodwork. On one side stands a 1920s gold fountain from a South Philadelphia funeral home. On the other a wood sleigh bed, and all around a Madonna and a trio of nudes floating above the ocean, and the mottled plane trees and the black and gray sky outside the window. It is here that the aging artist looks like a giddy child. "This is why I like it here," he says, evocatively framed in the middle of his room. "It could be anywhere," he declares, reciting the artist's conceit of self-invention.

It's possible to imagine that artists are a kind of societal avant-garde. They anticipate the future, break obsolete and arbitrary boundaries, forge connections. Chimes would say artists gaze back and forward at once, and what we ascribe to the future also colors the way we imagine the past. Fallon and Rosof and many others see in the hordes of young artists the same spirit of city-building that so infused Rembrandt Peale and his peers, the desire to make something out of nothing. It's a powerful desire, one amplified when it is projected across and onto the street grid, when the art being produced transforms and reflects the city itself.

This hope for art was understood quite early in Philadelphia, when in 1872, a diverse lot of citizens who thought the industrial city ugly, fragmented, and uncultured invented the Fairmount Park Art Association (FPAA). "Before the Parkway, the Museum, the Planning Commission, the Art Commission, this really was city planning," says Penny Bach, the Association's director.

Bach is nearing the completion of the second major project since her term as director began. The first, *Form and Function*, asked a selected group of artists to find a suitable site for their work somewhere in the city. The project most notably produced Martin Puryear's gracious *Pavilion in the Trees* in Fairmount Park, not far from the Centennial District gardens, and Jody Pinto's beloved *Fingerspan* near the Wissahickon Creek.

Begun in the 1990s, the second project, *New Landmarks*, was designed to respond to community needs, engaging residents in the process of creating public art in and for their neighborhoods. Bach explains, "We started by asking communities what they wished to leave behind."

"Negotiation yields results," she says emphatically. The first result, according to Bach, is a "little marriage" between the artist and the community, a marriage that furthers social and community networks and produces a sense of accomplishment. Here is a response to a question posed earlier: How can residents be made to feel that development might enrich their lives? In *Form and Function*, at least, residents are asked to think about a legacy, an assignment that requires a positive and progressive-minded response. Defensive ideas don't hold muster. And the impetus is placed on neighbors to invent a project. Critically, the artist elevates the idea. But it is done as an act of partnership. Fear is removed from the negotiation.

As art transforms the city, the city transforms art. Among the interesting projects is one that takes place in North Philadelphia. Here, in the project prosaically called *The Church*

Lot, the FPAA and the social service agency Project HOME commissioned artists John Stone and Lonnie Graham, who is also acting associate director of the Fabric Workshop Museum, and novelist Lorene Cary to create a sacred space on the vacant lot left by a fire at St. Elizabeth's Church at 23rd and Berks Streets. St. Elizabeth's was an icon in a neighborhood that boasts rather proudly restored 19th-century rowhouses with elaborate brick and terracotta ornamentation, bracketed cornices, and little wooden "balconies" and awnings. The rebuilt Raymond Rosen housing project is adjacent.

On a bright, cold February morning the neighborhood is quiet. Though this small section of central North Philadelphia remains intact, many of the surrounding streets are empty; they seem to suffer invisible ruin. Stone, a sculptor, is tall and wears a terrific head of dreadlocks. Graham, bearded, is soft-spoken and kind. He is philosophic about the project. "It's a very basic idea," he says, "to give people ownership over where they live and what they do."

But Graham, who was a Pew Fellow in 2002, sees a special role for artists in the community-building process. "Artists—painters, photographers, poets—have a valid, tangible role as creative problem-solvers, a useful role. It's something that makes a lot of sense." Stone calls giving regular people a say in public art "psychological ownership. It's where a lot of artists forget. It's an ego issue." And so the sacred space they're planning for *The Church Lot* (as it is called), as with many of the pocket parks that Stone has planned in the neighborhood, is designed and built by children, the elderly, and teenagers.

The project also re-sanctifies a luminous room inside the still-standing rectory. The renovated space, which includes a white oak table built by the sculptor Doug Mooberry from a 300-year-old tree, as well as a frieze of text from a neighborhood oral history project and large-format landscape photographs of the neighborhood taken by Graham, will be used for community meetings. As a repository, it will also house the oral and material history of the neighborhood.

Stone goes on to explain that foreclosure and abandonment have left the neighborhood with vacant properties. "The community is required to deal with it," he says. But the St. Elizabeth's fire, which seemed suspicious, left a particularly brutal scar, and neighbors were left to mourn. The artists' response is sculpture of galvanized and stainless steel that, according to Graham, "will allow access to the [sacred] idea that remains about this place, a physical interaction with it." Bach believes the strength of the work lies in the trust between the artists, whose ideas are avant-garde, and neighbors, who, she says, invest the work with meaning. The collaborative process is a community-building feedback loop. As Stone and I leave the rectory, we pass Helen Brown, the community activist who is spearheading the project. Brown then grabs Stone's coat, hugs him warmly, and plants a loving kiss on his cheek.

It's an enormous kiss, a great embrace. Here, then, is a true power of art: to erase boundaries between people, to overcome the silent separations of race, class, and social strata. It is fitting that it takes place here, a place that has witnessed the disintegration—indeed, in light of the fire at the beloved St. Elizabeth's, the incineration—of so much that binds a community together.

Now we expect public art to repair the damage, to rebuild neighborhoods, to reassert our principles. It's most certainly asking too much, of course, but the expectation alone tells us a great deal about our wishes for the contemporary city: it has to engage us visually, but also emotionally and intellectually. A

University of Pennsylvania professor of architecture, Winka Dubbeldam, offers a useful metaphor for framing this urban possibility. In an interview she says that her firm, Archi-tectonics, isn't "into stylistic things, but deriving form from *performance*." Using this lexicon, we might think of a building that merely functions as passive. One that performs aids and enhances. It gives back.

In order for form to follow *function*, but also to account for various functions, Modernism as a discipline separates uses—a roadway from a sidewalk, a residence from an area of commerce. Performance-based architecture attempts to balance even contradictory functions with a smile and a wink. Thus, stylistically, function informs a restrained (modern) aesthetic, while performance is something that is visually more active and perhaps interactive. Dubbeldam and other contemporary architects face a challenge: balancing sometimes conflicting desires, needs, and functions in a way that makes everyone involved more productive and invigorated.

We might think the same way about the possible city. A city that functions provides shelter, transportation, and common ground for the production of culture and commerce. A city that performs also wows us, inspires, entertains, dazzles, and raises the specter of our consciousness. It is comforting and challenging, open and particular; it makes human life not just possible but extraordinary.

Designer Thomas Heatherwick's Rolling Bridge in London is a useful example of Dubbeldam's concept. The bridge crosses a canal behind Paddington Station. The bridge functions: you can cross it, and, if you're in a boat, the bridge will move out of your way. But in important ways it also performs: it moves silently, without cables, and in a tight space it moves entirely to one side. Instead of opening like a traditional drawbridge, it turns itself into a piece of steel and wood sculpture. When it closes, or rolls up, it becomes an octagon. Then it unfurls, like a spider opening its legs. It's such a performance that to accommodate spectators, officials roll up the bridge every day at noon, whether there is a boat to pass or not.

Heatherwick says that architecture not only shapes physical space, but also our experience in the space. *The Church Lot* similarly functions as both a neighborhood park and a piece of art. As a park, it performs by providing neighbors a sacred space, a realm in which they can connect with neighborhood history and memory. It is also a vital piece of art; it performs—by inviting in people and their stories, by fomenting neighborhood dialogue and prolonging its memory—and binds people together as part of a place. Plus, over time, it will change and evolve, in synch with the neighborhood itself.

The truth is nowadays in most things mere function leaves us bored; it's simply no longer enough. A static sculpture—or a mobile—might have once been welcome at 23rd and Berks. The community may even have chosen it. But it wouldn't have met their need to grieve, to reflect on their heritage, to capture their own community evolution. Nor would it have allowed them, in real and transformative ways, to project their dreams onto the cityscape before them.

A city cannot merely perform; it must also function. The rooftop garden inside Philadelphia's Kimmel Center for the Performing Arts was installed as a piece of performance. Simply for pleasure, it allows visitors to access the sky above. It has no function otherwise, and therefore feels to the somewhat bewildered user like hollow space. The rather spectacular glass-covered gardens inside the Bellagio in Las Vegas also perform. In fact, they delight. But like Las Vegas itself, a city that performs but doesn't much function, the gardens serve no urban purpose. The danger is implicit in the discussion of contemporary Las Vegas, a city whose skyline is entirely faked. There form follows only performance—and the show is slapdash, coarse, and not even ironic.

There is also a valuable economic lesson here, one that ought to be applied to the city's streetscape. A city that performs enjoys a far greater return on its assets than a city that merely functions. Turn the Benjamin Franklin Parkway, Philadelphia's Champs Elysée simulacrum turned speedway, into a grand pedestrian entrance to Fairmount Park (with thousands of bicycles available to take you into the park, a Ferris wheel, and lots of places to sit and play) and you'll quickly forget how well it functioned as an expressway. In a city like ours there's little return on functional efficiency, but a great deal to profit from the engaged pedestrian.

The same functional impulse that produced the present configuration of the Parkway results frequently in the tearing down of old, historic, and suggestive buildings simply because they are in the way. There is play and contrast in the urban landscape that performs; there is morbid regularity in the cityscape that merely functions. This is an old notion, but we give it contemporary relevance out of necessity. If Philadelphia continues to underperform, devaluing its assets, the city will become too poor to even function.

One critical factor of Philadelphia's underperformance is that because it doesn't always physically cohere, it cannot dazzle. So often the city seems small when, in fact, it is huge; it seems stifling when it might be freeing; it seems homogenous when it is unendingly pluralistic; it seems fragmented and disconnected when it might be integrated and therefore broadly enticing. This is why, despite the enormous energy produced by artists across all parts of Philadelphia, the city as a whole doesn't feel like an art town. The art lover has to search, often without a guide. Few, for example, know of the Tiberino museum.

Philadelphia's neighborhoods are charming places with related but discreet histories, with traditions, with life cycles and daily rituals and institutions. Neighborhoods perform, usually in subtle and rhythmic ways, for residents. So in Powelton Village many people know when the Tiberinos are throwing a party. But few neighborhoods beyond Center City perform for outsiders. Few people come to Norris Square to go shopping under the El.

But the growth of Center City is changing that. Center City initially grew, beginning in the 1950s by filling in, and then, beginning in the 1970s, by spreading in all directions. Parts of what used to be South Philadelphia and North Philadelphia and West Philadelphia are now, in practice, Center City. Paul Levy, who has run the Center City District (a business improvement district), which markets and advocates for downtown since its founding in 1991, says that younger, more affluent residents who have colonized the border neighborhoods now expect the urbanity and delirious intensity of downtown living.

By following the contours of this shift, and hoping to create a higher-performing Philadelphia, one might invent an expanded Center City, which has as its northern boundary Norris Street. Morris Street might become the southern edge. To the east the Delaware River; 48th Street north to Girard Avenue would mark the western border to include the Zoo. What are now the neighborhoods of University City, Fairmount, Francisville, Brewerytown, Pennsport, and Passyunk Square would then be part of this 12-square-mile center. Perhaps the best justification for the change is the importance of physical scale and connections. The best connector of all is Center City.

Imagine it as a compass: it points in all directions; small in size it takes you only so far; much larger its capacity to connect has grown substantially—out into the middle band of turn-of-the-century Philadelphia, Walnut Hill in West Philadelphia to Passyunk Avenue in South Philadelphia to Swampoodle, Nicetown, and Germantown, and over to Kensington.

The act of invention is, in part, simply re-labeling. But critically it would also direct changes in criteria for density, height and use of buildings, parking, transit, and lighting. Center City more than functions: it is a legible place; signs and maps are clear, plentiful, and instructive.

At a very practical level, expanding the range of legibility invents a larger city. But 12 square miles, of 135 in all of Philadelphia, is still a short range, and so it is necessary to heighten connections all the way through.

A short anecdote is instructive. The campus of Philadelphia University is a wooded park on the slope that rises from the east bank of the Schuylkill River. The geography in this part of the city separates the campus, which includes the old Ravenhill Academy, where Grace Kelly attended school, from the East Falls neighborhood, indeed from the city itself. A walk from the East Falls Regional Rail Station to the Ravenhill part of the University is short, but it brings the unwelcome pedestrian to an unmarked hill at the rear of the campus.

The 32 bus, on the other hand, delivers the rider to Schoolhouse Lane and Henry Avenue, the University's front door. The bus also connects the campus to Fairmount Park, Boathouse Row, the Benjamin Franklin Parkway, and City Hall. The route ends quite near the Italian Market. Yet few students, staff, or faculty use it. Why this is so is a result of a handful of factors, including the lack of a bus shelter; it's also an indicator of how SEPTA falls short of the transit system required by a city that performs.

Philadelphia's transit system seems inadequate in comparison to other cities because it is based on the bus. Bus lines don't translate well to conceptual maps and they lack a physical presence, which means they are hard for most people to grasp. A subway system, on the other hand, has stations, stops, and maps so conceptual they simplify city life. And a subway station is a natural place to disseminate information. It is also manned.

But in most of Philadelphia outside of Center City, there is the ephemeral bus itself and, at each stop, nothing more than a small, rectangular card with the route number. At Schoolhouse Lane and Henry Avenue that card is posted 10 feet high on a telephone pole. There is otherwise no information about the route, its important destinations, or its frequency of service.

Now we might imagine the corner with a bus shelter. By providing lighting, shelter, and advertising, it will function. The best bus shelters also perform, by making the transit system and the city itself more legible. Stand at Schoolhouse Lane and Henry Avenue. It feels a little like standing in the middle of the woods. Where can you go from there? What's out there? Ask the policeman on the corner. Better, a bus shelter will tell—at every hour of the day; it brings the city alive. Here is the physical presence the invisible system needs, and what's more, the information required to inspire.

A bus shelter might also perform as a piece of public art, a way to engage artists in the streetscape that so often captivates them. This was just the idea that informed the artist Pablo Tauler's colored glass and steel bus shelters, installed on Chestnut Street between 7th and 17th Streets. His use of colored glass and vernacular building shapes turns a functional item into one that hints at something sacred.

Happily, the cost of installing and maintaining bus shelters is typically paid by advertisers—enough to return revenue to the city, too. Therefore the most formidable obstacle to installing bus shelters at scale throughout Philadelphia is the electrical hookup needed for lighting and the LED displaying on-time information. A Canadian firm has perfected a solar electrifying system used now in a quite cloudy Edinburgh, Scotland. There is an upfront cost to the solar system, which is installed without disturbing current infrastructure, but that cost is insignificant compared to a conventional electrical connection.

Quite as important as its impact on the individual bus rider, installing smart, perhaps evocative bus shelters at scale throughout the city is a formidable way to reject Philadelphia's default parochial position. At once, and at minimal cost, a larger, more accessible, more clearly connected city has been invented. It is open and easy to understand.

The world's only statue of Charles Dickens, Frank Elwell's *Dickens and Little Nell*, stands in Philadelphia, in Clark Park. Dickens himself, who liked Philadelphia but found the grid boring, was a great walker in the city. He lived for and absorbed the city's intensity (we might say the city performed for him). Writing in the first half of the 19th century, he was especially intrigued by the urban night. The simple streetlamp—lit with whale oil—had transformed the city into a stage. Dickens called the resulting spectacle the "magic lantern":

> It is as though [London's streets] give something to my brain which it cannot do without if it is to work ... I wrote

very little in Genoa and thought I had avoided traces of its influence—but, good God, even there I had at least two miles of streets by the lights of which I could roam around at night, and a great theater each evening.

I'd like to call the streetlamp the stage light of the urban night. But until a decade ago, Philadelphia had all but abandoned the streetlamp in favor of the cobra-style highway light that is designed to illuminate the road and not the sidewalk. Today there are some 100,000 of these lights throughout the city. In almost all cases they cast the wrong kind of light in the wrong place, effectively making the city seem ugly, fragmented, and less safe.

The cobra highway light, so named for the curving shape of its neck, was introduced in 1957 by Westinghouse just as the Interstate Highway Act was passed. The lamp they called the Silverliner became the most popular street and highway lamp in America. Why? Because it functioned so well. Normally posted 20 to 40 feet above the ground, the cobra highway light was designed to make driving safer. But most cities, new and old, installed the cobra everywhere: on shopping and residential streets and alleys, on boulevards and parkways. In old cities like Philadelphia, doing so meant removing cast-iron and wooden streetlamps and replacing them with aluminum posts. Because the new lamps cast so much light, they could be installed on just one side of the street, thereby saving municipal funds. The lamps were efficient and easy to maintain.

At the highway scale, the cobra light is symbolic of the way the driver is valued over the pedestrian. The light bathes the carriageway, but often leaves the sidewalk itself simply dark. Now imagine turning a cobra light 180 degrees around. It becomes a magic lantern. Now it lights the sidewalk; and now the city performs.

City for people, Lewis Mumford wonders, or city for cars? In a classic *New Yorker* Skyline column from 1963, "The Highway and the City," an angered and precise Mumford predicts every destructive result of the Interstate Highway Act. "For the current American way of life is founded not just on motor transportation but on the religion of the motorcar," he writes, "and the sacrifices that people are prepared to make for this religion stand outside of rational criticism."

"Every urban transportation plan should, accordingly," he says, "put the pedestrian at the center of all its proposals . . . But to bring the pedestrian back into the picture, one must treat him with the respect and honor we now accord only to the automobile...It is nonsense to say that this cannot be done in America, because no one wants to walk."

Paul Levy began reassessing the "city for cars" a decade ago when the first new sidewalk lamps were installed—and the first cobras were unceremoniously toppled. Since then his agency has installed nearly 2,100 lamps. (In this regard Levy is a contemporary Rembrandt Peale, who was an inventor of the gas sidewalk lamp, installing them at scale in Baltimore.) Levy's vision was immediately illuminating, and Center City was all of a sudden pleasant to be in at night. Soon, the lighting program was expanded and other agencies and institutions followed. The University City District, which has installed 300 lamps, is adding 84 more along Baltimore Avenue just beyond *Dickens and Little Nell*. The University of Pennsylvania adopted a shorter Center City hybrid lamp, Drexel University one that can be described as the "arms in the air" lamp, and other parks, bridges, institutions, and public spaces quickly followed suit. Since

1998, Philadelphia has replaced some cobras with an estimated 4,000 pedestrian-scale streetlamps.

All this has changed the performance of the Philadelphia night in certain locales. And once the city performs, it's hard to face mere function. So now a cobra-lit street feels wrong: mottled, dark, uncertain, and sometimes, as in my own block, inappropriately bright. The lighting has to be right. When it isn't the problems of the streetscape are only amplified. When it's inconsistent and fragmented, when the block you are on is well-lit but the next one isn't, the city seems to fall apart. The uncertainty is telling, especially in winter, when darkness falls at 4:30. The air is chilled and SEPTA is often inadequate at night. The sidewalk, betrayed, is empty. The shopkeeper can't make it—every aspect of city life suffers, but unnecessarily. It isn't that cold out.

There are four sets of railroad tracks and the remains of Lubinville to pass on the way from *The Church Lot* to Nicetown, the dollop-shaped neighborhood just below Germantown. And not a proper streetlamp in site. Here, often enough, life seems to suffer without end.

And yet when one searches the city for a place marked by ruins but open to invention, a place that desires elevation, a place that sees benefit in openness and connectivity, that rejects a disquieting parochialism, Nicetown emerges. It is worth careful consideration, for it is reinventing itself not just as a functional place, but rather as one that performs.

It is here in Nicetown that Stephen Hague stands on the open back porch of Stenton, the modest English estate built in 1730 by James Logan. Logan, a polyglot Quaker, was William Penn's secretary. He managed the colony, negotiated with

Native American leaders, and founded Pennsylvania's first substantial library. Hague has been Stenton's executive director for seven years. He has sandy hair and an easy but precise demeanor. His diction is slow and careful, his words modest. But after spending an hour on a luminous April morning discussing the framing of history—its uses, limits, challenges, and hopes—in the context of uncertain North Philadelphia, his diction has quickened. It isn't history that has excited him. Rather Hague seems inspired, inventing a future for Nicetown and Lower Germantown. "There is a lot of opportunity here," he says, then pauses. "And a lot of opportunity for missed opportunity."

Stenton, in the brochures one of the earliest American colonial estates, is really a window onto almost three centuries of a changing city. The view through the window includes Nicetown, built mostly between 1880 and 1920 for skilled factory and railroad workers and foremen, which today fits the archetype of urban decline.

"How do you think about a historic site in a deflated part of the city?" was a question Hague was asked to consider when he took the job. "Stenton was widely regarded as a special place in Philadelphia," he says, "but at the same time there is a big fence around it—a house built by a white man who had enslaved Africans living there." Stenton sits on a small parcel within a park and playground managed by Philadelphia's Department of Recreation. Stenton's three acres (shrunken from the original 500) are separated from the recreation center by a fence and maintained by the National Society of the Colonial Dames of America in the Commonwealth of Pennsylvania, which took over the property in 1899 as one of the nation's first house-museums.

The house was never severely altered from its original configuration, so it looks and feels much as it did in the middle of the 18th century. Indeed, one of the pleasures of Hague's tour is the realization that the rooms don't use electric light. As we come to a dark room, Hague enters first and opens one or two shutters, drawing light inside. This sort of magic draws several thousand visitors a year. Logan's 2,681-volume library, so critical to the intellectual development of the New World, was in a large, second-floor space that was also used for bedrooms. Logan left the books to the City of Philadelphia, and today they are in the collection of the Library Company. There is only one surviving bookshelf (of possibly 20) on display. Yet the room in its raw proportions speaks. "This is what we call 'the wow moment,'" says Hague of the room's power to articulate the combination of Quaker modesty and ambition that was so intrinsic to the formulation of America.

Hague's first action was to reevaluate the history told at Stenton; curators have since begun to amplify the story of women who lived there, particularly the early Philadelphia historian Deborah Norris and Dinah, a freed slave who is credited with saving the house from destruction during the American Revolution.

His next step is instructive of one way Philadelphians are inventing their city. Like the city's artists, Hague sought to build connections—with schools and neighborhood residents—and create networks among the dozen or so historical sites nearby. A grant led to the development of the History Hunters Youth Reporter Program, a collaboration of Stenton and three historic houses in Germantown. With the goal of making local history relevant to neighborhood children, History Hunters draws particularly on William Penn's life and ideas, Germantown's historic pluralism, and its uneven history regarding slavery (the nation's first anti-slavery position was proclaimed there in

1688). The program's lessons use the streetscape, public places, and historic houses to teach writing, math, history, business, and critical thinking.

History Hunters has led to further collaboration with other historic sites. Among the 14 organizations that comprise Historic Germantown Preserved there is, as Hague notes, "an incredible richness, the capacity to tell all kinds of stories." Collaboration also creates economic power. Here, again, it becomes apparent that function is no longer sufficient. Just as *The Church Lot* is a park that also performs, "historic sites are devices," he says, and assets that until now haven't produced an ample return to the neighborhood.

Nicetown is divided twice—by Germantown Avenue and the Roosevelt Expressway—and otherwise hemmed in by CSX and Norfolk Southern and SEPTA's Regional Rail tracks. A handful of "Winter King" trees grow just below the Expressway nestled at the edge of Nicetown Park, where it gives off to the highway on one side and the neighborhood on the other. There are three wonderful things worth noting about that tree, a hawthorn variety: its pale gray bark, its goblet shape, and its fiery berries. The first two—the bark and the shape—form a composition as moving as an olive tree in a Sicilian field (minus the blue of the Mediterranean); the third is the glory: clusters of red berries as certain of life as the first cherry blossoms of spring.

"I love these trees," says Majeedah Rashid, the Chief Operating Officer of the Nicetown Community Development Corporation. Rashid comes across immediately as a person to trust. She is honest about the neighborhood's prospects and at the same time it's impossible not to recognize her enthusiasm. Her eyes burn as brightly as the sun trapped inside the hawthorn berries. Her certainty is convincing.

The organization was started in 1999, with Rashid hired in 2002 in part to try to stitch the neighborhood back together. The Expressway, particularly, has left a tear in the urban fabric. "When I started here, I looked on old maps," she says, walking below the highway. "These were all streets. Cayuga ran right there."

Since then, the organization has commissioned three planning studies. "We have to keep it real," Rashid cautions. "Our first priority is to stabilize the commercial area." Rashid talks with her hands and to illustrate she's pushing them gently down, as if to say "a little at a time, a little at a time." She's wise enough to realize that it's impossible to reverse 60 years of decline with smart ideas. Rashid is also careful to traverse the political field. It's clear she had some success with former Mayor John Street, whose curfew program the Nicetown organization has made into a beacon of community trust. "We love it—it's absolutely working," she tells me, especially because it has fertilized positive relationships among adults, youth, and the police. But she's overjoyed with prospects for Michael Nutter's administration. "He's something else," she says, and smiles giddily.

Nicetown Park, with an iconic contemporary sculpture on Germantown Avenue, is the neighborhood's central public space. A few years ago, Rashid moved the August Nicetown Festival there; now the Community Design Collaborative, lauded by Rashid, has produced a pair of plans to improve the park and other neighborhood areas under the Roosevelt Expressway. Her favorite idea—"a concept so beautiful," she says—is to build a skate park using the existing highway pylons. When a neighbor originally suggested the idea, it wasn't well received. But he persisted and finally the task force assembled to work with the Collaborative's design team came to see the skate park as a way for the neighborhood to build on its strengths, turning an obvious liability into a source of pride.

The Nicetown Community Development Corporation will build a four-story, 37-apartment complex on Germantown Avenue, one block from the neighborhood's transit hub, the Wayne Junction Regional Rail Station. The complex will have three retail spaces and a community center. The design will meet some green goals. The funding for the project is much in place. "I'm telling you, it's going to be the catalyst," says Rashid, presenting herself as a visionary planner.

But Rashid recognizes that in a poor neighborhood particularly, mere function will no longer do. It doesn't inspire. Like the highway overpass that will be adapted as a skate park, her neighborhood, she believes, is going to have to perform if it is going to survive.

Wayne Junction Station was built in 1881 and rebuilt under the eye of architect Frank Furness in 1900. Then it contained a waiting hall and a baggage room, which is now part of the headhouse entrance on Germantown Avenue. The station, which also includes a 1930s tunnel across freight tracks, is on the National Register of Historic Places. It's a gem of the bourgeoisie, as is so much of the area: exotic rowhouses with inlaid decorative crests, generous porches, front gardens, and lampposts. The view west of the station is dominated by the late Victorian Glen Echo carpet mill, evocative and still used for industry. Just beyond, where Wayne Avenue heads into Germantown Avenue, the streetscape is formed by blocks of boxy, stick-Victorian single and twin houses and the colorful Zeralda Street.

Now SEPTA will spend $20 million to restore the station, a project that has Rashid thinking not only about stitching her own neighborhood together, but, more profoundly, about the openness and possibility that will result: the power the restoration proj-ect will have to sew Nicetown to Germantown—and the entire area to Center City. Here the city is being invented; as a different, larger, more open city, it will do much more than just function.

"For us," says Stenton's Hague, "[really good] public transit would be terrific."

But at present the station feels less like an asset and more like a barrier. "Our people don't even use it. They're afraid," says Rashid. (Despite this legitimate perception, ridership at the sta-tion is rising, by 27 percent from 2005 to 2007.) Safety, above all, drives the station renovation, says SEPTA project manager Rusty Acchione, a veteran agency engineer. Acchione, who grew up in Germantown, is gregarious and straightforward. He wears a Villanova class ring and neatly trimmed hair. He explains how his view of the project changed when, standing on the station platform, he witnessed a murder just below. "The neighbors are telling me, 'We love our station, but we're not comfortable using it.' We want people to use the station."

Six Regional Rail routes run through Wayne Junction, though not all trains stop. Enough do, however, to make this one of the few Regional Rail stations to be able to operate some-thing like a subway, where the rider doesn't have to depend on a schedule, especially if heading south toward Center City. SEPTA trains in both directions stop here 188 times a day; that's some-what less than the 271 Broad Street Subway trains that stop at Hunting Park Station, on the east edge of Nicetown. A Regional Rail train from Wayne Junction arrives at Market East Station in Center City in just 12 minutes, however—slightly faster than the subway from Hunting Park to City Hall.

SEPTA's plan will make the station function. In addition to making Wayne Junction compliant with the Americans with

Disabilities Act and installing an elevator, raising the "inbound" platform, integrating the "outbound" R7 platform, and renovating the station house and ticket office, Acchione wants to make the five station entrances and the walkways to the platform feel safe. That means cutting four- to five-foot site lines, improving lighting, and, in the case of the Germantown Avenue entrance, removing the historic headhouse, a brick and stone building with carved relief and terracotta tile roof.

Acchione's hope is that by removing the headhouse, the station will function better. The engineer also justifies his approach by citing the cost of renovating the headhouse, which he puts at $750,000. "What can I do for the station with that money?"

"There's lots of ways of addressing safety and security besides knocking down a beautiful building," Hague says. More critically, he sees the headhouse as an opportunity to bring real life into the station, one which is irreversible once the wrecking ball arrives. Old buildings perform in different, often more evocative ways.

One of the shortcomings of the Wayne Junction project is caused by SEPTA's infamous bureaucratic divisions. Acchione is charged with repairing the station. Someone else is in charge of Regional Rail scheduling (Does it make sense to run more trains to and from a revamped station?), someone else oversees bus operations (Is there a strategy to move riders off the slow 23 bus and onto the fast Regional Rail?), someone else manages the three neighboring maintenance yards, someone else promotions and advertising, someone else station maintenance (Wayne Junction is notoriously dirty, and there is no maintenance plan for the station once it is renovated), and someone else again the ticket office operations. All of these separate functions inform the overall project, but in Rashid and Hague's hopeful scenario, each function would follow a larger vision for the station as an economic engine.

"This is not pie in the sky," insists Stephen Hague. But if vision—and not bureaucratic division—is to lead, it will require more than a philosophy change at SEPTA. A renovated station will function better. Ridership will continue to increase. But in the possible city, Wayne Junction inspires, dazzles, performs.

The elevated platform faces the Victorian Glen Echo mill complex; together the station and the mill make a moving composition. It feels special, a place that fires the imagination. Just a few blocks away, through the ruins of an old factory, stands Stenton. Here, at the gateway to Germantown—for its richness and beauty one of the most compelling destinations in America—one might encounter the very firmament of the American experiment. The worst of it and the very best. Here, Penn's ideals were put into practice. Here, a visitor, if he can stomach the unpleasant walk between the station and Logan's house, will find in the first salon on the right a wampum belt much like the one given William Penn by the Lenape. It was, they say, a gift of friendship, an offering that would consecrate Philadelphia as a place like no other the world had ever seen. A place built on love, a place that elevated the highest instincts of humankind. It's here. It's all still here—and it's ours. What kind of city shall we make it?